# KNOWING GOD'S WILL

## PAUL MILLER

YOUTH WITH A MISSION

HARPENDEN

KINGSWAY PUBLICATIONS

EASTBOURNE

Biblical quotations in the main text are from the New
International Version © International Bible Society 1973,
1978, 1984, published by Hodder & Stoughton; and in the
preface from the New American Standard Bible © The
Lockman Foundation 1960, 1962, 1963, 1968, 1971, 1972, 1973.


*Front cover photo: Tony Stone Photolibrary— London*


Youth With A Mission (YWAM) is an international movement
of Christians from many denominations, united in Christ and
dedicated to presenting him personally to this generation.
Youth With A Mission,
13 Highfield Oval, Ambrose Lane, Harpenden,
Herts AL5 4BX. (Tel 0582 65481)

**British Library Cataloguing in Publication Data**

Miller, Paul
Knowing God's will.
1. Christian life
I. Title
248.4

ISBN 0–86065–671–3


Production and printing in Great Britain for
KINGSWAY PUBLICATIONS LTD
Lottbridge Drove, Eastbourne, E Sussex BN23 6NT by
Nuprint Ltd, Harpenden, Herts AL5 4SE

# Contents

# Foreword

I first met Paul Miller in Afghanistan fifteen years ago. He was a new Christian, fresh from the Himalayan mountains of India where he found Christ.

Paul lived with us in Afghanistan for over a year. We became fast friends, and over the years to come we also became co-workers in Youth With A Mission.

I have watched Paul grow as a leader and a Bible teacher. He is a man of great depth and integrity, and besides, he has a wonderful wit!

Paul has wrestled for years with the subject of divine guidance. He is not a man to accept superficial Christian jargon at face value; he questions until he finds answers.

This book is the fruit of Paul's search for wisdom and balance in the area of divine guidance over many years. It is one of the most balanced, practical and biblical presentations available.

Do you want to hear God's voice, with certainty that you are not just listening to yourself?

Do you want to know how to know God's will?

Do you have questions about why things you thought were God's will did not come to pass?

This is a book that will answer these questions, and many more!

I highly recommend it to you!

*Floyd McClung*
*Amsterdam, Holland*

# Preface

'God, after He spoke long ago to the fathers in the prophets in many portions and in many ways, in these last days has spoken to us in His Son. . .' (Heb 1:1–2). So with confidence the writer to the Hebrews affirms that the message of God is now complete. What more is there to say? His Son, Jesus Christ, is the first, last and complete Word (Jn 1:1,14), all other communications being subsumed and fulfilled in him (Jn 5:39; Mt 5:17). Having retained and preserved this message in the Scriptures (Lk 24:27), what more is there to be done but with the mind, acknowledging the Holy Spirit, we study these inspired writings (2 Tim 2:15)? When the results of this study are then applied, we will have people walking in obedience to the divine counsels, loving Christ by obedience (Jn 14:15); people living under the Word of God. Thus the whole duty of man is fulfilled as he orders his life according to God's Word in his Son, enshrined in the written word.

However, within three chapters the writer of Hebrews is exhorting us to hear God's word today. 'Today if you hear His voice. . .' (Heb 3:7). It is true he quotes from the Bible (Ps 95:7). but he is referring to the situation of his readers at the present time. Will they hear what the Holy Spirit is saying to them? The God who did a lot of speaking until Jesus came has not presumably lost his voice for 2,000 years, but is still wanting to communicate to us day by day. 'He who has an ear, let him hear what the Spirit says to the churches' (Rev 2:7). John the apostle still wants to know this even though he has touched and handled the Word of life Himself some years after (1 Jn 1:1). So God's Spirit speaks to our spirit in a 'still small voice' (1 Kings 19:12), of intuition, of a 'picture'— formerly called a vision!—maybe a dream, a word of knowledge, wisdom or prophecy, or perhaps even a tongue. As we move into the exciting world of the living God, what place or time of inclination have we for the staid cerebral intellectualism of study and expositions? The former picture of a diligent enquirer into the Scriptures appears too dry, formal, intellectual (that's not me!) and boring when God is waiting to speak specifically to us today! So the word of Scripture, though penned through the Holy Spirit (2 Tim 3:16), is relegated to second place, if not altogether neglected, in favour of the Spirit's voice. The mind of man—a prominent theme of the New Testament—is demoted and even abused as the necessary price for spiritual intuition, reception and revelation (Eph 1:17).

We all know that this dichotomy ought not to be. Scripture versus Spirit. Mind versus intuition. 'Logos' (written logical word) versus 'rhema' (spoken or breathed word). (Although this last distinction is generally true, it is not possible to maintain it definitively from the use of these two words in the Bible.) Paul Miller's book will help Christians of different traditions and experiences to appreciate and honour one another rather than to fear and separate. The twin fears of dry, orthodox intellectualism and wild extravagant claims of infallibility born from 'hot lines' to deity must be countered and qualified so that together we can know the whole mind of God.

Greater still is the contribution that Paul's book will make to the sensitive area of guidance. It will be the rare 'advanced saint' who will read these pages and not feel he has gained some clearer insight into ways God leads us through life, and Paul couples this with downright common sense and a sense of humour—both senses are necessary if we would walk humbly with our God (Mic 6:8)!

A mind renewed in spirit (Eph 4:23) and saturated in the Holy Spirit's Scripture—together with a clear inner man filled by the Holy Spirit—if placed amongst a group of those who 'love Thy law' (Ps 119:97), and 'worship in spirit and truth' (Jn 4:24), should not find that God's guidance is elusive, mysterious and uncertain. Rather, such a privileged believer will be able to affirm with David, 'My steps have held fast to Thy paths. My feet have not slipped' (Ps 17:5), and, 'Surely goodness and loving kindness will follow me all the days of my life, and I will dwell in the house of the Lord forever' (Ps 23:6).

Let's hurry on then into the chapters of this helpful theme, and better still into the adventure of a life ordered and led by the Spirit of the living God.

*Roger Forster*

# Part One:

# Revelation

# I

# *The Saved Who Are Lost*

'What is God's will for my life?' You've asked it. I've
asked it. We've all asked it. Does this question bother
you or bless you? You know, of course, that God has a
plan for your life, but you may be unsure as to how he
will communicate this plan to you. Are you certain of
your Christianity, yet unsure of God's will? You are probably clear about your final destination—heaven—but
your problem may be the stops on the way. Are you part
of the saved who are lost?

There is hope. God is committed to communicating his
will to us. This communication is vital. In wartime, cutting
the enemy's lines of communication is standard strategy.
If you can isolate and confuse your enemy you are halfway
to defeating him. So it should come as no surprise to
find the devil employing this very tactic against us. He is
working to cut off our communication with our heavenly
Father. But God is at work keeping the lines of communication open. In this book we shall be looking at the varied
lines of communication that God has made available and
discovering how to use them.

We all need guidance in our lives. A man I once knew
had a fear of being surprised by a burglar, which is natural
enough. But his special dread was that he would be
surprised without his shoes on. Minus his shoes he felt

more mouse than lion. (I suppose he felt terribly vulnerable with his toes exposed.) We feel much the same when we are unsure of how solidly we are standing on the will of God for our lives. When our foundation is shaky we feel exposed, vulnerable to fear and doubt.

Our desire to know the will of God for our lives is, of course, completely biblical. The apostle Paul prayed out this same concern for the believers of his day, 'asking God to fill you with the knowledge of his will through all spiritual wisdom and understanding' (Col 1:9). The great apostle would have voiced a similar concern for the 20th century church. With Paul, we need both prayer and wisdom if we are to pass from the 'problem' of guidance to the 'promise' of guidance.

The promises of guidance are abundant. 'The Lord is my shepherd . . . he leads me' (Ps 23:1–2) is the Bible's promise and the Christian's comfort. A shepherd that neglects the guiding of his sheep is a mere figurehead, which is a position King Jesus will never settle for! He is not an absentee landlord content only with the position but shunning the responsibilities entailed.

Jesus reinforces the promise of Psalm 23 when he says in John 10:14, 'I am the good shepherd.' In John 10:3 it is mentioned 'He calls his own sheep by name and leads them out.' He would hardly be a good shepherd if he didn't lead them out. What else does a shepherd do if he doesn't guide and lead his sheep?

Isaiah 58:11 says, 'The Lord will guide you always.' That is a pretty categorical statement. It doesn't say, 'The Lord *hopes to* guide you'. It says, 'The Lord *will* guide you'. And notice the word 'always' rather than 'most of the time'. For whom is this promise? The verse could not be clearer here—it says 'you'. The promise is not reserved for the super-sensitive, superspiritual, supersonic saints of old who were specially plugged into God. It is for ordinary 'Joe Bloggs-following-Jesus-as-best-I-can'-type Christians. In other words, *you*!

Proverbs 3:5–6 says, 'Trust in the Lord . . . lean not on your own understanding . . . and he will make your paths straight.' Here we have both a wonderful promise and a clear command. The command directs us to a source outside ourselves—it directs us to God. Decision-making time is always 'leaning' time. We'll either lean on our own experience and understanding or we'll lean on God's. Leaning on God's guidance is not optional for the Christian. Dependency is the name of the game.

Our God hasn't just left us to our own devices to 'get on with it as best as we can'. On the contrary. As a popular evangelistic tract has put it: 'God loves you and has a wonderful plan for your life.' For many Christians, this important truth creates as many problems as it solves. Our difficulty lies not in believing that God has a plan for us, but in discovering what in the blazes it is! We see the promise and the goal but we are not altogether sure we know how to get there. We wonder, 'What is his will for my life, and how will I recognise it when I find it?' These are big questions which must somehow be grappled with, because a wonderful will for our lives that is unobtainable and can't be known doesn't do us much good. It is as helpful as knowing that there is plenty of money in the bank but that none of it is in our account. It just leaves us more frustrated. It could be compared to the proverbial carrot before the donkey. That may be how men motivate donkeys, but it's not how the Good Shepherd guides his sheep!

Unfortunately, anxiety over guidance is more likely to plague the sincere disciple than the lukewarm, which doesn't mean that anxiety is a mark of spiritual zeal. It's just that the cold-hearted Christian is, by definition, less concerned to know and do God's will. When you combine sincere desire with uncertainty about God's methods of guidance the unhappy result is agonising self-doubt, hesitation and crippling indecision. We muddle through as best as we can, doing what we feel we must do, but in the back of our minds lurks the gnawing fear that we have moved 'out of the Spirit' and made a decision 'in the flesh'. If someone were to ask us whether we were quite certain that we had found and done God's will, what would we reply? We'd shrug our shoulders, shuffle our feet, study our shoes, nervously clear our throat and feebly squeak, 'I hope so.'

No wonder, then, that we find guidance a problem. We react like many a non-Christian who, upon being told that the living God has a will for their life which needs to be found, exclaim, 'Oh, I've enough problems on my mind without having to worry about that!' This anxious attitude hardly seems to be the intended fruit of the earlier quoted Bible passages on guidance. Peace and security seem rather to have been the aim. Something has gone wrong in our understanding of guidance.

There must be a way of combining both zeal to do God's will and peace as we go about it. Jesus had such a consuming passion to do his Father's will that he said, 'My food is to do the will of him who sent me and to finish his work' (Jn 4:34). Yet anxiety never seemed to dog his steps. We must find his secret.

## The Bible's place

'But surely', you may say, 'we have the Bible to solve our problem of finding God's will?' Well, yes and no. That is, the Bible does give us authoritative revelation in the areas of doctrine ('Who is God?' and 'How do we get right with God?') and ethics ('What is right and wrong?'). However, our problems in guidance are not usually in these areas of cosmic ultimates, but in the smaller, practical decisions of life. My dilemma as a Christian is not whether I should go out and murder someone today, but whether I should go out and witness to my neighbour today. My confusion lies in wanting to know if God wants me to buy that new car, or move to that new job. Does

God have anything to say to us in these areas? And where are we going to find God's opinion about the new car when the Bible doesn't even mention cars? So often we are faced with decisions entailing not just right/wrong, but good/better/best.

Our anxiety level shoots up when we hear such maxims as, 'The good is the enemy of the best.' 'Oh no,' we think. 'You mean it's more complicated than just finding and doing what is right and good?' Because what separates the 'good' from the 'best' is not morality (for the good would not be good if it was immoral in any way). The Bible's clear commands on right and wrong do not help us here; it does not tell us directly whether being a doctor or being a mechanic is best. Where then do we turn?

The Bible does tell us where to go in these circumstances, and it is with this conviction that this book is being written. The Bible does not say, 'I have come to analyse your problems and to dissect them abundantly.' It moves beyond analysis to solutions. But the solution is not to see the Bible as some kind of comprehensive workbook wherein can be found specific answers to every possible question. If you are wondering whether you should be a doctor, you cannot look in a Bible index under 'doctor' and expect to be directed to the relevant page where detailed information can be found on the kinds of Christians who can be doctors. The Bible does not answer all these questions, but it does show us where we can go to get them answered. Just where to go for these answers is the concern of this book.

### Anxiety antidotes

Two effective antidotes to anxiety are trust and understanding. A book cannot feed you intravenously with the needed dosages of trust, but it *can* nourish your understanding. Increased understanding of the ways of God provides a foundation for trust to develop.

Trust focuses on God's willingness and ability to guide us rather than on our inability to hear him. When we trust, the fact that God has 'got it together' looms larger than the fact that we do not. If the Bible speaks the truth, then God is more willing to guide us than we are to be guided. The initiative in guidance is with God.

The apostle Paul, busily instructing and directing the new churches under his care, was undoubtedly grateful that he could fall back on a God who actively gave guidance. If Paul failed to get through to his charges, his world did not collapse because he knew that God was there and was communicating. He wrote to one group of disciples saying, '. . . take such a view of things. And if on some point you think differently, that too God will make clear to you' (Phil 3:15). His confidence was in a God who was not passive in the area of guidance. Is yours?

Trust focuses not only on God's willingness but on his ability to guide. 'Yes, of course,' we say but how many times do we secretly feel that the real blockage to guidance is our inability to hear God. We're often too spiritually thick, but consider the spiritual thickness of those pillars of our faith, the twelve apostles, and be encouraged. Even after three years of intensive training Thomas had not grasped the basics. We find him at the Last Supper confessing that he did not have a clue where Jesus was going off to, never mind the more complex question of the way there (Jn 14:5). What is encouraging is that this spiritual dullness did not prevent Jesus from being able to guide them. It will not stop him from guiding us either.

Understanding is also a key antidote to anxiety. It is as we clearly understand what is expected of us and what we can expect of God that anxiety is dispelled. 'I have told you these things, so that in me you may have peace' (Jn 16:33). Peace comes as we listen to God. He not only communicates his orders but also his understanding. 'I no longer call you servants, because a servant does not know

his master's business. Instead, I have called you friends,
for everything that I learned from my Father I have made
known to you' (Jn 15:15) Understanding is a part of being
a son of God. Ignorance is not at a premium in the
kingdom. The Holy Spirit continues Jesus' 'making it
known' ministry (Jn 16:14). Thus we have confidence that
as we cry with Moses, 'Teach me your ways so I may
know you' (Ex 33:13), we are praying in the will of God.
We need to understand his ways of guidance.

God leads us through four main channels:

1. The Bible.
2. The Spirit.
3. My own judgement.
4. My own creativity.

In the Bible—God's letter to us—95% of God's will for
us has already been revealed. If we are serious about
knowing and doing the will of God we need to study and
heed this book. There are so many good books tackling
the theme of the Bible's place in the Christian's life and
how to study it that we will not be addressing it in the
course of this book. Suffice it to say that it is of utmost
importance. So important is it that the list found above
could well be laid out this way:

1. THE BIBLE

2. The Spirit
3. My own judgement
4. My own creativity

The Bible is not just a way that God guides, but it is the
main way that God guides. It stands supreme when it
comes to communicating God's will to us. But God also
communicates in other ways.

Chapters 2–4 of this book will examine the place of the

Holy Spirit in guidance. Chapters 5–7 will deal with the
place of reason. Chapters 8 and 9 will look at the place
of creativity and human initiative in guidance. Each
chapter will be a self-contained whole so that you can
skip to whatever chapter you find helpful without needing
to read the previous chapter. In this way, should you find
it unnecessary to read, for instance, the chapter justifying
the belief that God speaks by his Spirit, you can skip
straight to the next chapter detailing how he speaks and
how to listen to his Spirit. Just read what helps you.

## Rational and mystical

Notice that I have made a place for both the Spirit and
our minds in this scheme of guidance. This book is dedicated to the proposition that the mind and the Spirit, the
rational and the mystical, belong together. In the creation
God moved mysteriously by his Spirit, but he also acted
rationally, planning everything out in minute detail. If he
had not said, 'Let toes have toenails,' they would not
have had them! What God has put together (the rational
and the mystical) let no man put asunder, or it will 'put
us under' spiritually. God works both through our rational
and our 'supra-rational' faculties. He wants us to both
listen to the voice of his Spirit and to use our logical
minds. We will be studying the proper roles of these
rational and mystical approaches in Chapters 2, 3 and 5.
In Chapters 2 and 3 I shall fight hard to establish a legitimate place for God speaking by his Spirit today. Then
in Chapter 5 I shall fight equally hard for a place for our
rational minds.

This viewpoint will be important to us as we look at
what is 'spiritual' in regards to guidance. Are you confident when it comes to guidance that you are 'walking in
the Spirit' as scripture commands (Rom 8:4)? Would you
say you are being 'led by the Spirit' (Rom 8:14)? Can a
spiritual Christian afford to use his mind? Can he afford

not to? If we are not confident at this point it is all too easy for condemnation to set in. Our lack of confidence may be due to a misunderstanding of the interplay between our minds and the mind of the Spirit. Clarifying this interplay, then, becomes vital. Chapters 5 and 6 will do exactly that.

## Practical and theoretical

We will be looking in future pages at the practical question of what to do to find guidance. We will also be looking at the theological, biblical justifications for the views I'll be putting forward. Both approaches are essential. We need the practical 'how-to's if the teaching is to be applied to our lives and make any difference to the way we live. And what is teaching for if it's not to be applied?

How did Jesus teach? That's always a good question. He gave very practical, 'how-to'-type advice even on such personal, sensitive matters as prayer. When the disciples asked him how they should pray Jesus did not trot out a long list of 'deeper principles'. He essentially said, 'Just copy this prayer. Say after me, "Our Father... ." That's it, you're getting it.' He gave them something very concrete to do. He didn't just give them something meaningful to think about. We need some of this same approach in learning about guidance.

There is the danger of oversimplifying the 'how-to's of guidance. This can only further an unhealthy technique-oriented type of Christianity. Read the right 'how-to' book and presto, you think you can do it. It's as easy as one, two, three. This approach neglects the fact that our walk with God is a relationship, not a technique. Nevertheless, just as there are helpful 'how-to's for meaningful relationships, there are also helpful guidelines for guidance. Rather than replace the need for a deeper relationship with God, they can show us what course to pursue in order to have one.

Yes, we need to know the practical 'how-to's. But we also need to know the biblical reasons for our views and actions. Indeed, there is nothing so practical as good theory. Just look at our modern world which is built upon myriads of scientific theories. We want the 'why's as well as the 'how-to's. Why do I believe God can speak today? Why do I believe I can simply make up my own mind on issues? Am I certain? If we are not convinced that we are approaching our decision-making biblically we will surely be unable to implement our approach wholeheartedly. And the promise of finding God comes to those who seek him with their whole heart (see Deut 4:29). If we are not convinced our approach is biblical we can hardly expect to seek God in faith. But the condition to God rewarding our seeking is: 'And without faith it is impossible to please God, because anyone who comes to him must believe that he exists and that he rewards those who earnestly seek him' (Heb 11:6). Our beliefs in these areas have very real practical implications. It is crucial, therefore, to settle just what we believe and why we believe it.

## Conscious and unconscious

So far we have been discussing consciously received guidance. Not to be ignored is the truth that God also guides us unconsciously. There are a whole host of decisions about our lives that we never have to make because God takes care of them. How many of us agonised over what century we should be born in or over what sex it would be most advantageous for us to adopt?

As in the big matters, so it is in the smaller affairs: God is there too! See David's encounter with Goliath, his first stepping stone into the ministry God had for him (1 Sam 17). He just 'happens' to meet him in the course of his daily, humdrum errands. And what about Joseph; was he told step-by-step his next set of instructions? No, he seemed rather to be at the mercy and whim of circumstances (Gen 37–41). Where was God in all this? And where was his promised guiding hand? He was there, but it was only clear in retrospect. Afterwards, Joseph could say, 'So then, it was not you who sent me here, but God' (Gen 45:8). His guidance was there, but it was hidden in the circumstances.

I doubt that mighty, worldly Caesar Augustus would have said that God had guided him to decree a census of the entire Roman world. But God surely did, because the census fulfilled the prophecy that the Messiah would be born in Bethlehem (Lk 2:1–4, Mt 2:3–6). Caesar was guided without being aware of it.

So relax! If a pagan Roman seeking world domination can experience God's guidance, surely a believing Christian seeking God's will can too. The guided Christian life is not a life of strain, a life where we need always be impossibly alert, fearful that a moment's relaxation will result in missing what God wants to say. No, there are many things God guides us into without us even being aware of it.

Nevertheless, it is still true that God wants to guide us consciously. Neither Jesus nor the apostles simply stumbled through life blithely unaware of God's intentions or directions for their lives. The book of Acts is not only a record of people doing the works of God, but also a record of people consciously following the leadings of God. 'The Spirit said' is a recurring phrase in the book.

We have seen already that the apostle Paul prays for believers to be filled with the knowledge of God's will (Col 1:9). Notice that he not only wants them to do God's will but to know it. The God who never changes wants the same for us today.

# 2

# *He Is There and He Is Not Silent*

You may have heard the story of the Christian student who went off for a weekend house-party with some friends. To his dismay he found that this was a house-party with a difference: there was to be no talking all weekend outside of the teaching and worship sessions. Fed up with this by Saturday afternoon, he decided to take the afternoon off shopping in town. So while the afternoon Bible study got underway, he slipped out of the room and crept down the hallway. Triumphantly he turned the corner only to bump into the retreat leader! Surprised to see him, the man asked him where he was going. Flustered but quick-thinking, the student replied, 'The Holy Spirit has led me to go shopping in town this afternoon.' The older man responded to this: 'Well, of course then, you must go. But I hope the Holy Spirit and you know that it is half-day closing!'

There is scarcely any truth more susceptible to abuse than the truth of divine guidance. If even a quarter of those claiming to be led by God were telling the truth, then God has been the author of everything from innocuous hair-brained schemes to heinous mass murders. 'God told me to do it' runs a close second to 'The devil made me do it' as the most popular excuse for our human misadventures. But because a thing has been abused is no basis to dismiss it outright. There are many who would reject all religion and 'God-talk' with the rationale that it has been the cause of so much hate and bloodshed. Others would reject the Bible on the same basis. Should we as Christians then avoid this controversial God and stay away from our Bibles? This is poor thinking indeed! Let us not use the same line of reasoning to reject the Holy Spirit's work of leading and guiding us. We need to let the Scriptures rather than people's negative experiences inform our thinking. The resulting outlook on hearing God's voice will be positive and expectant rather than cautious and hesitant, for this is the scriptural outlook.

*He Is There and He Is Not Silent* is the name of a book written some years ago by the late Francis Schaeffer. The title admirably fits the theme of this chapter. God wasn't silent 3,000 years ago in early Israel, he wasn't silent 2,000 years in the days of the Acts, and neither is he silent today. The God who communicated to Abraham, and who personally spoke to Moses, is the same God who directs our lives. Centuries of constant communication have not worn him down. He has not hived off to some peaceful retreat where he can refrain from the wearisome task of conversing with man. He is the God of the living and he is ready to talk . . . to you.

We want to reclaim from the lunatic fringe the precious truth that God speaks today. This was never meant to be a truth reserved solely for the wild-eyed fanatics, the self-styled Jeremiahs, and the pale, ethereal mystics floating three feet above reality. It was always meant to be a part of 'normal' Christianity. What is normal is set out in the Bible.

In this chapter and the next we want to establish the normality of being led by the Spirit of God who speaks to us. This means that we shall be looking at different biblical passages in some detail, as well as examining the broad sweep of Scripture. This desperately needs to be done because a common objection against the 'charismatic' wing of the church is that it shuns the earnest study of the Scriptures; that its beliefs are founded on personal experience rather than on the eternal, unchanging truth of the Bible; and thus that its doctrines are shallow and not to be taken seriously.

Is guidance by the Spirit of God a doctrine based soundly in the whole message of the Bible, or is it based on a few flimsy proof texts? Is spoken guidance exceptional, rare and not to be relied upon, whereas written guidance (the Bible) is normal and reliable? A two chapter walk through the Old and New Testaments should soon answer these questions.

## Guidance in the Old Testament

The Old Testament is inexplicable without a 'speaking' God; that is, a God who communicated through the spoken word as well as the written word. As a matter of fact, without God's spoken word there would have been no written word—how would the writers have known what God was saying? Without a speaking God there would have been nothing to write about. Without a speaking God Moses would have died in Midian smelling of sheep. There would have been no mighty miracles, no crossing of the Red Sea, no manna in the wilderness, no book of Exodus. Each new development in Moses' saga is initiated with the phrase, 'Now the Lord spoke to Moses.' (See Exodus 6:1,13; 7:1, 8, 14; 8:1, 16, 20; 9:1, 8, 13; 10:1, 21; 11:1; 12:1; etc.) We get the idea . . . the Lord said something to Moses! The repetition would be almost tiresome were it not so important. God spoke!

The Jews' glory and distinguishing mark was that they had both God's presence and his written principles. ' "Surely this great nation is a wise and understanding people." What other nation is so great as to have their gods near them the way the Lord our God is near us whenever we pray to Him? And what other nation is so great as to have such righteous decrees and laws as this body of laws. . .' (Deut 4:6–8). In effect, Moses is saying to the people, 'Hey, you are unique.' Unique! 'Yea, positively eccentric and weird,' some sceptical soul mutters. But no, their uniqueness was not in their oddball behaviour; it was to be found in the reality of God's activity among them.

The Jews stood out firstly because of the wisdom of their laws. These were the principles ruling their lifestyles which we find recorded from Genesis through to Deuteronomy. These laws were fixed, immutable. The Jews didn't need to go afresh each day to inquire of God how to sacrifice or how to treat their neighbour. God had spoken once and for all. Secondly, the Jews stood out not only because of their wise laws given by God in the past, but because God was real to them in the present. The passage in Deuteronomy says that God was 'near them'. This is not meant in the sense of Acts 17:27–28 where God, being present everywhere, is near all mankind, Jew or Gentile. He is near the Jews specifically in the sense that he responds to their prayers. His nearness is seen. He concretely acts and specifically guides. They could specifically seek him, and he would answer specifically. This is how God wanted to reveal himself to and through the Jews. This was not meant to be a one-off exceptional occurrence just during Moses' lifetime. God meant it to be a permanent characteristic marking them off as the people of God.

Where there is life there is movement and expression. Where there is life in personal beings—whether that personal life be human beings or the Creator God—this life expresses itself through speaking and doing. The God of the Jews was vibrantly alive. Jehovah differed radically from the idols of the surrounding nations 'which cannot see or hear or eat or smell. . .' (Deut 4:28), 'They have mouths, but cannot speak. . .' (Ps 115:5). Jehovah could and did speak. Life always expresses itself.

In a passage full of meaningful insights A W Tozer has written,

> The greatest fact of the Tabernacle was that Jehovah was there; a Presence was waiting within the veil. Similarly, the Presence of God is the central fact of Christianity. At the heart of the Christian message is God Himself, waiting for His redeemed children to push in to conscious awareness of His Presence. That type of Christianity which happens now to be the vogue, knows this Presence only in theory. It fails to stress the Christian's privilege of present realisation. According to its teachings, we are in the Presence of God positionally and nothing is said about the need to experience that Presence actually . . . for the most part we bother ourselves very little about the absence of personal experience.[1]

Hearing God speak is one part of knowing the reality of God's presence that Tozer is speaking about, and the Bible is full of it.

Without a speaking God, who could explain or even excuse the actions of a Noah or a Moses? Would you have wanted to identify with this Noah character? What if he had been a member of your church? Can you see yourself explaining to your neighbour what he was doing in his backyard constructing that ridiculously large boat. Not only Noah, but your church would have been the laughing-stock of the town! If you had asked Noah what occasioned his sudden nautical interest his answer would not have involved weather charts and earthquake readings. His simple answer would have been, 'God said.' Does that sound flimsy? That's all right. A flimsy truth is better than a solid falsehood.

What about Moses? Did he have some eternal principle written on stone to guide him? Was there a prophecy written down in Genesis saying: '. . . and out of Midian shall come a deliverer, both a prince and a shepherd, a son of Levi shall he be of three score and ten years'? Not in my Bible. Again, it was simply that 'God called to him. . .' (Ex 3:4).

Then we have to consider Abraham. Is his life explicable solely in terms of written principles? Not at all. How would you have counselled somebody who walked up to you, nervously wringing their hands, and blurted out: 'God has appeared to me. He has spoken that I should kill my son!' Dubious, you begin your counselling session by asking for background material. You then find that he has a history of this kind of thing. Yes, he claims he was led by God some seven years earlier to pack his wife and fourteen year old son off to wander alone, defenceless in the desert (Gen 21:11–14). What biblical principles can you conjure up to produce that sort of guidance? It was the God who speaks who directed Abraham in this way.

Then consider King David. He actually believed that God spoke into the nitty-gritty of life and not just about the more universally important, earthshaking matters. So he inquired of the Lord as to the specific strategy to use for a specific battle. And the Lord answered him specifically (1 Sam 23:2, 4, 11, 12). The result was success in the battle. Surely the Lord is just as interested in speaking into the nitty-gritty of our lives as into the details of King David's life.

Conversely, we see Joshua's failure in dealing with the Gibeonites. The specific reason given for his being taken in by their deception was: 'The men of Israel sampled their provisions but did not inquire of the Lord' (Josh 9:14). They made a commonsense decision on the basis of past experience and present information, and they were wrong. Their mistake was not that they ignored the written principles of the Word. Their mistake was in neglecting God's present-day voice. As the saying goes, 'It's not what you know, but who you know.' And they weren't going to the One they knew.

A booklet has been written entitled *Your Mind Matters*. The appropriate reply, of course, is, 'Yes, but God's mind

matters more.' The problem with Joshua was that he
knew his own mind, but ignored God's.

Continuing our stroll through the Old Testament we
come to 1 Samuel 3:1: 'In those days the word of the
Lord was rare; there were not many visions.' Clearly the
tone of this comment does not convey approval. Rather,
it betrays the low spiritual state of Israel. The priests of
Israel had been unfaithful, and God was displeased. With
Samuel on the scene the whole picture brightened visibly.
God began to communicate again in a living way.

Note that the word that was rare was not the written
word. Banish from your mind any thought that the
problem here was that a severe depression had hit the
printing business in Israel ('People just aren't buying
books any more!'), or that a chronic shortage of papyri
was drastically reducing the output of Bibles by the
normally efficient Hebraic Bible Society. No, this passage
refers to a shortage of God's spoken word. God inspired
the Scriptures, but he evidently wanted to speak outside
of them. Has he changed today? I can find no scripture
that says he has.

God has always had a living voice. Throughout the Old
Testament he spoke directly to his servants. What do we
see in the New Testament? Is it possible that the riches
of the old covenant could be greater than the riches of
the new covenant? Could the Jews before Christ have
enjoyed more of the demonstrated presence of God than
Christians today? Do we have to settle for a God who
has withdrawn himself? Let's look and see.

**Guidance in the New Testament**

In the New Testament John the Baptist is galvanised into
action as 'the word of God came to John . . . in the
desert' (Lk 3:2). This does not mean someone sent him
a Bible for his birthday! No, he heard from God! He was
obviously told it was time to start preaching. It wasn't

that John the Baptist stumbled upon a verse in the book
of Haggai where to his surprise he found these words: 'In
the fifteenth year of Tiberias Caesar one John, son of
Zechariah, shall go up to the Jordan'. How did he know
then? God spoke to him.

What about Jesus? Like John, Jesus did not just operate
on the basis of principles learned from the written word.
He moved on the basis of current, divine communication.
'The Son can do only what he sees his Father doing. . .'
(Jn 5:19). He was not only led by what he had read but
by what he saw the Father currently doing. 'I judge only
as I hear. . .' (Jn 5:30). Notice that he says 'hear', not
'read'. Jesus does not seem to be speaking about making
decisions on the basis of principles learned from reading
Scripture alone. Hearing God speak played a key role.
(Please do not take this out of context; remember what
I said about the importance of Scripture in Chapter 1).
We see an example of this in Luke 4:1: 'Jesus . . . was
led by the Spirit in the desert. . .' He was not moving on
his own whim or even on biblical instructions, but rather
on the guidance of the Holy Spirit.

What about the early believers? The Book of Acts is
full of accounts of the early church following in Jesus'
footsteps. Indeed, what does a disciple do if he doesn't
follow in his master's footsteps? So the apostles did the
same deeds as Jesus and heard from the same Spirit as
Jesus. Philip struck up a conversation with an Ethiopian
eunuch because 'The Spirit told Philip, "Go. . ." ' (Acts
8:29). The key to understanding how a stuck-in-the-mud
Jew like Peter could actually reach out past the level of
his scriptural understanding to embrace the fact that God
could save Gentiles comes when we realise God could
speak. 'While Peter was still thinking about the vision,
the Spirit said to him, "Simon . . . go. . ." ' (Acts
10:19–20). The great apostle Paul's crucial travelling
ministry was initiated not so much through solid Bible
exegesis, but by a direct word from heaven. 'While they

were worshipping the Lord and fasting, the Holy Spirit said, "Set apart for me Barnabus and Saul for the work to which I have called them" ' (Acts 13:2). Can we not take these passages to be saying what they appear to be saying, that God spoke by his Spirit?

And can we take these apostolic experiences as examples for us? Are they examples to be emulated, unusual experiences to be admired? Jesus' clear instructions on the teaching and guiding role of the Holy Spirit show us that we can expect the same. We were not meant to direct our lives solely by our unaided human intellect, even if this intellect is feeding on the Bible. Revelation— divine communication—is also necessary.

In John 14–16 we have the most concentrated, clearest teaching Jesus gave on the work of the Holy Spirit. As one reads through these passages it becomes clear that the Holy Spirit's brief is communication. He heads the Ministry of Communication, a key department in God's cabinet. His work is described in the following terms: 'The Holy Spirit . . . will teach you . . . will remind you. . .' (Jn 14:26). 'The Spirit of truth . . . will testify about me. . .' (Jn 15:26). 'The Spirit of truth . . . will guide you into all truth . . . he will speak . . . he will tell you. . .' (Jn 16:13). The Holy Spirit is a communicating Spirit. Through constant repetition Jesus kept hammering home this point. It must have been important to him. Hear again what Jesus said about the Holy Spirit: 'He will speak.' Do we believe it? Could it be that simple? Does Jesus mean what he apparently is saying, or is he hiding his meaning behind a phrase we think we understand? Did the 'speak' of these verses mean 'not speak' in the original Greek? What do you think?

Some may object, saying that the truth the Holy Spirit promises to guide us into is the truth of already revealed Scripture. They would object to applying this truth to what we call 'guidance'. Let us allow Scripture to interpret Scripture. What sort of truth do we see the New Testament church being led into? It is true that we see the Holy Spirit giving the apostle Peter insight into Scripture. In Acts 1:15–22 he sees from the written word the necessity of replacing the twelfth apostle. In Acts 2:16, on the day of Pentecost, we see Peter being given insight into Joel's prophecy. Yet in Acts 8:29 (the Ethiopian eunuch), 10:19 (the Gentile enquirers), and 13:2 (Paul and Barnabus sent out), the Holy Spirit speaks to the disciples not about Scripture, but about current situations. In these situations, were the disciples being led into truth? The answer, of course, is, 'Yes!' (This is especially clear in Acts 10 where Peter is seeing the truth that God accepts Gentiles.) Was it the Holy Spirit who was leading them into this truth? Yes! Then it would seem valid to conclude that the above are all instances of Jesus' promise being fulfilled that 'The Spirit of truth . . . will guide you into all truth' (Jn 16:13). This means that this promise relates to current life situations in which we need to know God's truth and God's view.

The Holy Spirit is not confined in his remarks to a book written mainly between 1400 BC to AD 100. He is not only found between two black Moroccan leather covers. He has a few things to say here and now. As well as being a rich, living Bible commentary, he is a life commentary. He will not only help us exegete our Bibles, he will exegete our life situations. Not only could he give Peter insight into a Hebrew scripture (Acts 1:16, 2:16), he could also give Ananias insight into a real live, up-to-date Hebrew man called Saul (Acts 9:10ff). The Spirit not only gave a perceptive grasp of the Scriptures in the original Greek, but he also gave a perceptive overview of the original Greeks themselves (see Acts 18:9–10).

Some may object to applying the promise of Holy Spirit guidance in John 16:13–15 to all Christians. They might consent to the scope of the 'truth' being wider than just written Scripture, but they would say it is misdirected to apply this promise to anyone beyond the original apostles.

At this juncture it would be helpful to remember that even before the apostle Peter was spectacularly led to the truth that God accepts even the Gentiles, some humble, ordinary Christians had been led to this same truth (Acts 11:20). It was not just the apostles who were being led into truth.

See how clearly the apostle Paul states in 1 Corinthians 2:10–16 that all Christians are recipients of the Holy Spirit's leading-into-truth ministry. It almost seems that Paul is paraphrasing John 16:13–15 in this Corinthian passage. He writes, 'We have not received the spirit of the world but the Spirit who is from God, that we may understand what God has freely given us. . . God has revealed it to us by His Spirit' (1 Cor 2:12, 10). Who are the 'we' in this passage? Is Paul merely referring here to himself and his apostolic cronies, or does he mean 'we Christians'? The context makes it clear that 'we' refers to all of us Christians. All of us need not only the objective facts of the gospel but a subjective revelation as to their real meaning.

To start the Christian life we need divine revelation. 'No-one can say, "Jesus is Lord," except by the Holy Spirit' (1 Cor 12:3). What Paul is making clear to the Corinthians is that we also need supernatural communication to continue our Christian walk. 'We have . . . received . . . the Spirit who is from God, that we may understand what God has freely given us' (1 Cor 2:12). The Holy Spirit continues his revelatory work after his initial conversion work. There is so much he wants to say that we cannot possibly get it all in one shot.

Some who deny that God still speaks in the way we have been talking about still want to give room to the communicating work of the Holy Spirit. They will call this work 'illumination'. 'Illumination' is allowed, while 'revelation' or 'speaking' is out. But this only avoids the real issue; it is mere word play. The issue is present-tense communication by God's Spirit and not what specific words we use—whether 'led', 'felt', 'sensed', or 'had illumined to me'—to describe this communication. Once we allow that God communicates today in illumination we have opened the door to the principle that God communicates outside of his written word, and that is the core of the issue.

John 10:27 is a passage which reinforces Jesus' specific teaching of John 14–16 on the place of the Holy Spirit communicating today. Jesus said, 'The sheep listen to his voice. He calls his own sheep by name and leads them out' (Jn 10:3). This seems to be a fairly clear promise. How wide is the scope of this promise? *All* sheep, Jesus said. This was not to be an experience reserved for the elite sheep or the original twelve sheep.

What is this 'voice'? Clearly it refers to God's spoken word via his Spirit and not just God's written word. The verse says, 'He calls his own sheep by name. . .' (Jn 10:3). Clearly this cannot be a function of the written word because there are many names not recorded in the Bible. If you are Chinese and are graced with the name Wang Mingdao, is God calling you by name? Most certainly he is. But you will search a long time, and in vain, to find Wang Mingdao in the Bible. How is God calling Mr Mingdao then? By his Spirit, of course, through the spoken word of God.

All of the above gives a sound biblical base to the conviction that God still speaks to his people in this day and age. So when Christians claim that 'the Lord told me' it is not necessarily a glib, unfounded remark. Nor can it be dismissed as evidence of an arrogance that would carve out for itself a special place close to God's throne with a unique 'hot line to heaven'. No, it is Scripture which tells us we have a 'hot line to heaven', and, in that case, it would be dumb not to use it!

In summary, it is a half-truth to say that when Jesus went to heaven he left us his words in the Scriptures. He also left us his Spirit. God has always given us his prin-

ciples and his presence. He makes his presence felt. He
is not simply a gentle, benevolent, unseen presence in the
background. He acts. He communicates. It was so in the
Old Testament, and it is so in the New Testament.

## Dangers on both sides

Isn't this a dangerous truth to advocate? I mean, aren't
we opening the door to a baffling variety of colourful
doctrines and hybrid revelations—half scriptural and half
demonic in origin—once we give a place to God speaking
today?

The truth is that there are dangers for both the 'Word-
oriented' believer and the 'Spirit-oriented' believer. Christians tend to divide into different camps. There are those
who are more 'into' the Bible, and there are those who
are more 'into' the Holy Spirit. The clear danger of the
Word-oriented Christian eager to catch the exact shade
of meaning in the original Greek is the pitfall of dead
orthodoxy. This is right belief without right practise. This
is a mind full of correct dogmas but a heart devoid of
correct reactions.

This was the Pharisees' problem. They diligently
studied the Scriptures but resisted the Holy Spirit who
was wooing them to come to Jesus. I quote again from
A W Tozer who wrote, 'Truth that is not experienced is
no better than error, and may be fully as dangerous. The
scribes who sat in Moses' seat were not the victims of
error; they were the victims of their failure to experience
the truth they taught.'[2] Understanding Scripture became
an end in itself rather than a means to an end.

This is a possible problem for us today as well. We
evangelicals are in danger of travelling the same path
the Pharisees took when we elevate the Bible above the
ministry of the Holy Spirit.

The danger for the more Spirit-oriented Christian hot
on hearing God's latest heavenly revelation and eager to

practise hospitality towards any wandering angelic visitor
is quite different. He is more likely to drift away from
the sure rock of God's written word into a mystical haze
of subjectivism. His own present experiences—and the
more spectacular they are the better—are set above
God's will revealed in the past. Seeking experience
replaces seeking God. If the pitfall of the Word-oriented
believer is a cold heart, the pitfall of the Spirit-oriented
believer is a hot head and an overheated imagination.
The ability to make cool judgements is lost; indeed, it is
seen as a sign of one's lack of 'spirituality'. This makes
the superspiritual, revelation cowboys impossible to
correct. One is dismissed as 'walking after the flesh'. And
so their error is secured. Beware! Heresy is only a step
away.

A quaint yet helpful formula is the following:

All truth      = Dry up
All Spirit     = Blow up
Spirit and truth = Grow up

We need both Spirit and truth in our worship and in
our Christian lifestyles. Jesus said the Pharisees erred
because they did 'not know the Scriptures or the power
of God' (Mt 22:29). In our lives we need both Scriptural
understanding for our heads, and the present power of
God in our experience; to know God's word revealed in
the past, and to know God's word spoken today by his
Spirit. Satan cares little if we go astray by way of the cold
heart or the hot head. Either way he wins.

## Why doubt then?

In the face of this very clear picture from Scripture, why
do people insist that the Holy Spirit does not speak today;
that we are not to look to him for direct guidance? It's
because they interpret their Bibles to say so. I suspect

that their interpretation is coloured by several factors
other than pure logic, such as:

1. *The absence of experience.* Not seeing many signs of
the supernatural in their lives, they reach for an interpretation that fits their experience.

2. *Negative experience.* They are repelled by the stories
of frauds who, claiming to be led by God, lead the gullible
up the garden path.

3. *The weight of tradition.* The theological tradition in
which we were raised or presently live also influences us.
We all live within 'climates of opinion', and none of us
are immune to the effects. Mainline Protestantism's
'climate' has been decidedly unfavourable to the supernatural, a climate which stems back to those staunch Protestant forefathers Luther and Calvin:

> Luther came to admit that no one raised the dead any more
> and that what passed for healing miracles seemed to him to
> be the Devil's artifices and not miracles at all. The day of
> miracles is past, he concluded, and the real gift of the Holy
> Spirit is to enlighten Scripture, for 'now that the apostles have
> preached the Word and have given their writings, and nothing
> more than what they have written remains to be revealed, no
> new and special revelation or miracle is necessary.' Or in
> Calvin's words, 'The gift of healing disappeared with the other
> miraculous powers which the Lord was pleased to give for a
> time, that it might render the new preaching of the gospel
> for ever wonderful. Therefore, even were we to grant that
> anointing was a sacrament of those powers which were then
> administered by the hands of the apostles, it pertains not to
> us, to whom no such powers have been committed.'

The influence of these two men can hardly be stressed too
much. Practically all Protestant theology begins from one or
the other of them. Whatever reason they had for rejecting
miracles—whether they were reacting to an emphasis in the
medieval church, humanism, or to the developing implications
of Aristotelian thought—makes little difference. Calvin and
Luther alike left the precedent that healing was a dispensation

for a former time, and the matter was settled for later 'orthodox' Protestants.[3]

They lifted up the Bible and cast doubt on any concrete, felt, heard or seen ministry by the Holy Spirit.

But did these Reformers in this instance get their theology from a fair reading of Scripture? Were they not, most probably, influenced by their overriding concern to refute the Catholic teaching on the key role the saints fill in our lives. A mainstay of the Catholic argument for their saints were miracles, the argument being that supernatural miracles indicated supernatural approval. By the simple expedient of denying that God did miracles today the Reformers could completely nullify this line of logic. The miracles could then only be classified as either fictional or demonic. But the cost of winning the argument in this manner is too great.

While we are not investigating the wider subject of miracles, the above quote is relevant to our topic in that Luther and Calvin's argument is not aimed at physical miracles alone but at God's voice as well. The Holy Spirit's role was to be confined to enlightening Scripture. He could not act or speak on his own independently of Scripture. In practical terms, the Holy Bible was lifted above the Holy Spirit. It is no wonder that someone has quipped that the evangelical trinity consists of: 'The Father, the Son, and the Holy Scriptures'!

To simply give a 'psychological' explanation for another's rejection of the supernatural would be unfair. It would be better to deal honestly with the scriptural reasons advanced for holding these views. That is exactly what I propose to do in the next chapter.

# 3

## *Objections, Your Honour*

In deciding the innocence of the accused, a jury is not to give a verdict until it has heard from both sides: the prosecuting counsel and the defence counsel. Only then can it give an adequate judgement. Having in the last chapter presented our case, we shall let the prosecuting counsel step up and present their case. We shall put our points in the dock and let them defend themselves. They ought to be able to stand; and if they cannot, then we had better leave them where they lie anyway.

Handling objections can be heavy work. We might find ourselves getting bogged down in this theology here or that Greek verb there. Still, just as some people enjoy the self-inflicted pain of jogging, some of my readers might enjoy the sport of 'bogging'. For those who tend to get lost in bogs of close biblical argument I will chart our course from the outset. If you are unhappy even with this guided tour just skip to the next chapter.

Here are the chief objections that I have found and which we shall address:

1. That the recorded instances of divine guidance in the Bible were exceptional experiences for 'special' believers, and are therefore not indicative of what we can expect in our own lives.

2. That it is a truth reserved for the first century 'apostolic age'.

3. That it is a challenge to the unique authority of the Bible.

4. That we are more mature today so we do not need to rely on this sort of Holy Spirit guidance.

We shall devote a section of this chapter to each one of these objections. At the beginning of each section I will lay out how I propose to deal with that particular objection. Then we will look at each point in more depth.

## Exceptional or exemplary?

The first and major objection to this teaching from the lives of the characters found in the Bible is that they were all 'special' believers; that they all occupied a special place in the outworking of God's programme. Thus it is ill-advised to take their experiences as typical for they were the exception rather than the rule. They were unique. When God did a miracle or spoke to them it was only because they were unique. We are reminded that 'you are not an Abraham, a Moses, a Daniel, or an apostle Paul'. Their experiences were one-offs and should not be seen as imitable by us.

My response to this criticism is four-fold:

1. The teaching that these experiences were unique and unrepeatable is nowhere clearly taught in the word, and surely this is a serious defect in any teaching that claims to be scriptural.

2. The Bible shows supernatural deeds and communication to be normal for God and normal for the New Testament believer.

3. This objection rests on a misunderstanding of the teaching-by-example method of Scripture.

4. While we would agree that Moses, Jesus, the apostles and others, were unique, their uniqueness was

not to be found in the reality of their contact with the supernatural.

In answering these protests we shall be ranging over scriptures that do not directly touch on 'guidance' but relate to the wider subject of the entire supernatural realm. This is because what is being objected to is the wider area of the supernatural. Divine guidance is simply a part of the wider picture.

## Where is it found in the Bible?

This is my first question. The absence of any clear statement to the effect that the supernatural is for the few is a serious shortcoming for a viewpoint which purports to be the true, biblical view. Surely one should be able to cite chapter and verse to back up interpretations of Scripture.

Our assumption should be that Jesus' teaching and example still holds good for today unless it is specifically revoked. Can you imagine the Israelites saying, 'We don't need to sacrifice animals anymore. That was only for the initial "Mosaic age" of the Old Testament. We are mature Jews now. Where does it specifically say that sacrifices are still applicable in the year 700 BC?' No, they obeyed the last thing God told them until he specifically told them otherwise. This is key to understanding the Bible. It is to scriptural exegesis what 'innocent until proven guilty' is to jurisprudence.

Some have thought that in 1 Corinthians 13:10 we have a scripture that says the supernatural has passed away. Paul says, 'But when perfection comes, the imperfect disappears.' It is claimed that the perfection referred to here is the full New Testament—the full Bible—and that the imperfection referred to is supernatural events like tongues and prophecies. But of course the perfection referred to is our full union with our God after all sin has been judged, when the first heaven and earth have passed away and God himself shall dwell with his people. It is at this time that we will see him 'face to face' (1 Cor 13:12; Rev 21–22). That is when we will not need others to prophecy to us because we will be able to talk to God face to face about it! (For that matter, we will not even need the Bible then.) No, neither this nor any other scripture tells us that God has ceased intervening in his creation.

If we are to conclude that Jesus switched tactics after his resurrection or after the first century and began to limit the extension of the supernatural to the few, we will need stronger scriptural evidence than a theology built on silence.

## Extending the supernatural was Jesus' point

The lack of specific scriptures limiting the supernatural to the exceptional is an even more serious shortcoming in the light of the whole thrust of Jesus' ministry to multiply his ministry beyond himself. He was extending the supernatural, not confining it. See his steps:

*The twelve*: They were his first target. In choosing them he was not looking for travelling companions to stave off the inevitable loneliness of life on the road. He wanted to reproduce his ministry through them . . . and he did!

*The seventy-two:* The circle widens. In Luke 10 we see the seventy two receiving the same supernatural commission as the twelve.

*Anyone:* John 14:12 provides the next link in the chain. Here Jesus promised that 'anyone' could walk in the miraculous. 'Anyone' is an all-inclusive word. There is no small print to this promise stating 'anyone who believes . . . and is exceptional, and was born between the years AD 30 and AD 100'.

*The world:* The circle then widens beyond Judea to the entire pagan world. Paul, in 1 Corinthians 12–14, does not warn the Corinthians against the supernatural gifts— especially tongues and prophecy[4]—but shows them how to exercise them properly.

This is the thrust of the New Testament: extending the supernatural to all rather than limiting it to the few.

## Examples are examples

An example is not a deed you admire but an act you follow. Are the deeds of Scripture merely admirable or are they imitable? Those who think them admirable say, 'You cannot get theology from the Gospels or the Acts. You must go to the Epistles for this.' They have a point, but the other side of the coin is that our Epistles-based theology must not negate the teaching in the Gospels and the Acts.

Jesus used a 'show me' approach as well as a 'tell me' style. His method of teaching was not just the more abstract, classroom method of the Epistles. Example was key, and this has always been true of God. We can see the teaching role of example in the following texts.

'All Scripture is God-breathed and is useful for teaching . . . and training in righteousness' (2 Tim 3:16). So *all* Scripture teaches us—not just the epistles. They are 'useful', which means it is practical material relevant for us today rather than just academic knowledge of how God performed in the past.

'These things happened to them as examples and were written down as warnings for us. . .' (1 Cor 10:11). We see here that God's dealings with the Israelites were not just for their benefit but as an example to us today. An example has no point if it has no application in the present. He is teaching us his ways in a non-classroom setting.

'For everything that was written in the past was written to teach us, so that through endurance and the encouragement of the Scriptures we might have hope' (Rom 15:4). The same point once more. All Scripture – the examples as well as the directly didactic material—is teaching applicable to us.

'Haven't you read what David did when he and his

companions were hungry?' (Mt 12:3). Jesus appealed to an Old Testament incident in showing the validity of his breaking the Sabbath. He not only saw the direct teachings of the Old Testament as being instructive for us, but the concrete events as well. Jesus seemed to have no qualms about getting theology from parts of the Bible that were not ostensibly teaching sections. He got a principle out of a historical deed.

'The words "it was credited to him" were written not for him alone. . .' (Rom 4:23). Here is Paul getting a theology of justification out of a life experience of an Old Testament character. Can I hear somebody saying, 'You can't get theology from the lives recorded in the Old Testament. For theology you must go to Leviticus or Deuteronomy'? But Paul seems to think he can glean theological truths out of the dealings and deeds of God as well as out of the sayings of God; that is, he seems to think they are examples for contemporary believers.

Applying all this to the area of guidance, when we read of God speaking to the old saints it is valid to deduce that this was written not for them alone but for us, that through the encouragement of Scripture we might have hope that God will speak to us as well.

God's mode of teaching was not purely academic. He not only taught by what he said—by sermons and abstract concepts. He also taught by what he did. Jesus used a 'show me' approach as well as a 'tell me' style. First, he did it and the disciples watched. Then they did it while he watched. Finally they did it without Jesus' supervision. Using the example of his own life was central to his method of training his disciples.

The entire Old Testament is a storehouse of teaching in the ways of God. Is teaching only to be found in those sections of Scripture which contain the Ten Commandments, or the exhortations of the prophets—in other words, the passages of Scripture which clearly teach? Can we not learn much from the lives of the Davids, the

Daniels, and the Joshuas? If not, then more than 50% of the Bible is just 'filler'! Is there a practical reason for the inclusion of so much biographical material in the Old Testament beyond showing us the historical roots of our faith? Or is God some sort of cosmic history professor saying to us, 'Isn't it interesting how I once behaved?' Obviously not; the Bible portions quoted above make that clear. Faithfulness to the Bible means faithfulness to biblical example as well as to biblical precept.

*Biblical characters are unique but. . . .*

Should the fact that 'we are not Moses, Daniel or the apostle Paul' dissuade us from expecting the same reality of supernatural communication that they experienced? No, this would be to confuse the callings of God with the dealings of God. Their uniqueness lay in their special callings and ministries, not in their divine connection. Others who did not have their unique ministries experienced supernatural guidance. Think of Zechariah, Ananias, Stephen, Philip, and others who were the less significant characters of Scripture.

Some would say that these are the exceptions to the rule. But there are too many exceptions for there even to be a rule. The exceptional is the rule! If we go so far as to say that everybody the Bible mentions is unique (therefore disqualifying them for example status) we are reduced to the ridiculous position where, instead of believing it because it is in the Bible, we don't believe it because it is in the Bible. The Bible becomes a rule for what we don't do . . . at least in the supernatural realm. Because people are in the Bible they are unique; so therefore we do not believe that what happened to them will happen to us. This hardly seems to be the role God intended for the Bible.

**An apostolic age**

Another chief objection is that miracles and God speaking to men was reserved for a special age called 'the apostolic age'. This is a very similar objection to the above except that it focuses more on a special time period than on special men. The men are only incidental; Peter or Paul are only special because they lived in this special age.

The chief characteristic of the apostolic age was that it was an age of new revelation. The New Testament was being formed. The argument goes that in order to demonstrate that the writers of this new revelation were indeed men of God giving God's message there had to be some irrefutable stamp of divine favour upon them. What more convincing method than miracles and other supernatural experiences? These called attention to and authenticated their message. But these supernatural displays are not to be thought of as the norm for ordinary disciples. Once this new revelation had been given and the writers passed away, miracles ceased. Mission accomplished.

This objection is weak on the following three counts:

1. This special apostolic age is nowhere specifically mentioned in Scripture. Only two basic covenants are spoken of.

2. The need to call attention to and authenticate the message of the Bible is equally as pressing today as it was in the first century.

3. Seeing the role of the supernatural to be solely that of demonstrating God's approval of the minister is inadequate. It is true, but it is only a half-truth.

*The Bible knows of just two covenants*

Once again we are forced to observe that this point of view is nowhere spelled out in Scripture. This should immediately set off some warning bells. Any doctrine that cannot be substantiated by the direct statements of Scripture should be held lightly at best.

Not only is the Bible silent about a special apostolic age, it actively teaches a quite different scheme of things. How so? Well, my contention is that those who hold to the belief in this apostolic age are actually saying that there are three distinct periods in God's timetable; the old covenant before Jesus, the new covenant after Jesus which we are in now, and an inbetween period (the apostolic age) where God expressed himself supernaturally. A covenant is known by the provisos and privileges it offers. The imagined privileges of this so-called apostolic age (miracles and God speaking directly) are so substantially different from the age in which we now live that it seems to stand apart as a separate covenant all on its own. But this is quite contrary to the biblical scheme of things where there are not three great covenants or timetables but just two (see Gal 4:24; Heb 9:1, 10:9).

The difference between the two perspectives of God's work could be laid out in the following charts:

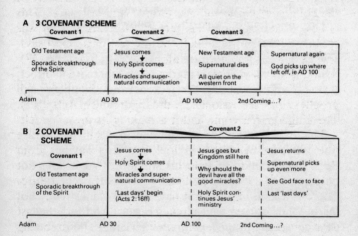

The first diagram shows a God retreating from active involvement in the world. The second chart portrays a God personally involved in the world. This would seem to be a better interpretation of Jesus' central message, 'The kingdom of God has come'. The King has come! He's here! Heaven has invaded earth! The good news was not, 'The kingdom of God has visited!' Jesus' plan was not to introduce the kingdom and then take a break for 2,000 years.

According to the first diagram the kingdom's coming is rather like a car which starts up with a confident roar only to lurch, cough and sputter for the rest of its journey. Is that the kingdom plan? Was it doomed to start well with an abundance of the supernatural only to lurch along without it for the next 2,000 years?

The Holy Spirit was to be the key to continuing kingdom work of Jesus. The day the Holy Spirit was given to the church at Pentecost was the inauguration of Phase B of 'Operation Kingdom Come'. It was the birthday of the church. It began the age termed 'the last days'. This is how Peter explained Pentecost: 'No, this is what was spoken by the prophet Joel: "In the last days, God says, I will pour out my Spirit on all people" ' (Acts 2:16–17). And this age, says Joel, is marked by an increase in direct, divine communication: 'Your sons and daughters will prophesy . . . see visions . . . dream dreams' (Acts 2:17). The kingdom has come and it is making its presence felt.

This is not the place to examine in detail the phrase 'the last days' as found in Joel, but it is obvious from Peter's application of it to his situation that it does not only apply to a coming millenial age far off in the future. There is a kind of 'last, last days' where things really hot up, but the last days have already begun. And with the last days comes the prophesying, seeing visions and dreaming dreams—supernatural communication!

## We need miracles equally today

The reasoning that there was an abundance of the supernatural in the first century because God was introducing new revelation and wanted to call people's attention to it and authenticate it holds equally true today. Is not the gospel just as much a 'new revelation' to the heathen Parisian or the Cambodian immigrant as it was to the people of Palestine? It makes no difference to them that the message is in fact 2,000 years old if in fact they have never heard it before. The first time you hear it it is 'new' to you.

And is the modern Englishman more ready to believe than the first century Palestinian so that he does not need the supernatural to convince him? If anything, the opposite is true. Surely the Bible needs as much heavenly authentication today as the apostles needed in times past.

## Paying attention is only half the game

While Jesus did miracles to gain attention to his role as Saviour, this was only half of his motivation. They were 'signs', but they were also expressions of compassion. What drove him to miraculously feed 4,000 people? 'I have compassion for these people; they have already been with me three days and have nothing to eat' (Mt 15:32).

Sometimes Jesus even expressly told people not to publicise a miracle he had done. He wanted them to keep it to themselves (see Mk 1:44). This is hardly the action of a man who sees the miraculous primarily in terms of a public relations exercise.

What relevance does this have for us today? Well, it means that God is still motivated to speak to us. If God's sole motivation was authentication of new revelation, once this new revelation had been completed then God would have no more reason to break into our world supernaturally. He wants to communicate with us not just to prove the Bible is true, but because he loves us and wants to talk to us and guide us.

## A challenge to the Bible's authority

It has been suggested that believing in continuing revelation today challenges the finished revelation of the Bible. Some warn us that this belief will downgrade the Bible as God's unique, final and authoritative revelation. After all, are some of God's words more authoritative than others? If God speaks today aren't we obliged to grant these words a place of authority equal to the Bible? And then aren't we dangerously putting our own subjective revelations on par with the Bible? Our personal Mount Sinais of today, where we get our own revelations from God, too easily become the Jonestowns of tomorrow.

Four responses are appropriate at this point:

1. It only threatens the Bible's authority if the Bible claimed that the Bible alone was the sole means of God communicating to man. My contention is that the Bible never makes this claim.

2. Saying that we will have to put our own revelations on the same par as the Bible misses the real point which is: Is God's authority equal to the Bible's?

3. Believing in God speaking today is not the doorway which leads to cultish beliefs. Not testing these 'revelations' is the doorway.

4. If this objection is correct then Scripture would undermine Scripture, and that does not make sense.

Firstly, I maintain that in no way is the Bible's authority challenged as it is the Bible itself which puts forward the notion that God can and will speak outside of the Bible. This is what we attempted to establish in Chapter 2. Rather than being a challenge to biblical authority, we hold this doctrine *because* of biblical authority.

If I sent you some messages via two office boys you would not see one as being in competition with the other,

or one being a challenge to the other. You would understand their work to be complementary. So it is with the
Bible and the Holy Spirit.

Secondly let's look at the rather perceptive question,
'Are some of God's words less authoritative than others?
If we hold that God speaks outside of the Scriptures
aren't we then driven to the disagreeable position that
our personal revelations must be on the same par with
Scripture? They must have equal authority, for are any
of God's words less authoritative than others?' My answer
is, 'Quite right, every word of God is equally authoritative, *but* . . . every word of God is not Scripture.' Can
you see the difference?

John 20:30 states, 'Jesus did many other miraculous
signs in the presence of his disciples, which are not
recorded in this book.' I presume that as always Jesus
was in communication with his Father during these non-
recorded occasions. Now, were these non-recorded
miracles any less supernatural than his recorded ones?
Was the communication Jesus received from his Father
at this time any less inspired or authoritative due to it not
being recorded in Scripture? And were any comments or
teaching Jesus did on these occasions less authoritative
than his recorded comments? Maybe that is why the
apostles left them out? Patently absurd! No, his words
and deeds were all equally authoritative and God-
ordained, but not all of them are 'Scripture'. So God
could speak with authority and yet his words not be Scripture. And God can speak to us with authority, and yet
these words would not be Scripture.

There is something fundamentally out of tune with
Scripture in this fear that the voice of the Spirit challenges
the voice of the Bible. It is not a fear that we see expressed
in Scripture. Can you imagine Abraham hesitating to
accept God's command to 'Go' in Genesis 12 because he
was worried that if he did he would be challenging the
authority of Genesis 1–11? He probably hesitated to obey,

but not for that reason. And did Abraham avoid God's command to him to sacrifice his son with the excuse that a spoken command from God compromised the authority of his written commands? I am sure he wished he could have. Was this spoken command authoritative for Abraham? Of course. On what basis? Not on the basis that it held biblical authority (it was not even Scripture yet) but on account of God's authority. God has an authority independent of Scripture. He gives Scripture its authority rather than Scripture giving God his authority.

The biblical characters gave room for God to speak with authority outside of Scripture. And they did not fear that this would undermine the authority of his written word. If it did not undermine it in Abraham's day it does not undermine it today.

I need to make two cautionary remarks at this point. First, we need to emphasise that the Scriptures are closed. Though God will speak to us with authority we are not involved in the revelation of Christian doctrine. The fundamentals of the faith have already been revealed. So if you think you are getting some new revelations on this score you had better re-check the source of your 'revelations'.

The second caution is this: the Bible is inerrant, whereas I am not. The Bible is God's 'sure word', whereas my revelations and guidance are less than sure. We are finite human beings prone to error. It is necessary to have a good, healthy sense of our finite humanity. The practical outcome will be that we will take our 'revelations' with a pinch of salt. I provisionally accept them, but with reservations and with the need to have them confirmed. This is not because God's spoken word is any less authoritative than his written word, but because I may have misheard his word.

Years ago A W Tozer wrote a little article entitled 'In Praise of Disbelief'. In it he wrote,

A bit of healthy disbelief is sometimes as needful as faith to the welfare of our souls. It is no sin to doubt some things, but it may be fatal to believe everything. Faith never means gullibility. Credulity never honours God. The gullible mentality is like the ostrich that will gulp down anything that looks interesting. I have met Christians with no more discrimination than the ostrich. . . . The healthy soul, like the healthy bloodstream, has its proper proportion of white and red cells. The red corpuscles are like faith; they carry the life-giving oxygen to every part of the body. The white cells are like disbelief; they pounce upon dead and toxic matter and carry it out to the drain. Thus the two kinds of cells working together keep the tissues in good condition.[5]

So let's have a bit of healthy disbelief in our own revelations.

My third response to this objection is that it is simply not true that we stand defenceless before false doctrine once we open the door to the possibility to God speaking today. The fear of deception is not groundless, only misplaced. The real culprit here is not a belief in God's current voice, but rather an insufficient grasp of Scripture. By exalting the current ministry of the Holy Spirit we are not saying that we do not also desperately need the written Scriptures. The basic reason people are led astray into false revelations—like the Book of Mormon or the Koran—is that they are not willing to submit these 'revelations' to the ultimate touchstone of truth, the Bible. Our personal guidance and revelations need to be submitted to God's written word. It is when we do not do this that we can get into trouble.

Do not throw the proverbial baby out with the bath water. The poor thing is getting bruised! To say that belief in extra-biblical revelation and guidance is the problem in heresy is like saying that the culprit in false teaching is the gift of teaching! How many people have been led astray by charismatic (in the natural sense) Bible teachers who forcefully present their particular view? Do we disallow the gift of teaching because of this abuse? No, the problem is not with the gift but how it is used. The problem is in not sufficiently submitting the forcefully presented truth to the scrutiny of the word of God.

Fourthly, if believing in Holy Spirit communication undermines biblical authority then the Bible is undermining itself! The same God who uplifts Scripture, saying, 'Scripture cannot be broken' (Jn 10:35), also uplifts the ministry of the Holy Spirit, saying, 'The Spirit himself testifies with our spirit. . .' (Rom 8:16). If present-tense, Holy Spirit communication undermines past-tense written communication, then you cannot allow even the 'testifying' that Paul refers to in this passage. Perhaps this too was only a first century, apostolic experience! Why should a little bit of Holy Spirit 'testifying' be innocent, but a modicum of Holy Spirit 'speaking' be threatening? If a principle is correct it will apply across the board. A belief in guidance does not undermine the Bible.

## More mature today?

There are some who say that we Christians have 'come of age' since the old covenant days. We are more mature because we have the full revelation of the complete Scriptures today and therefore do not need the detailed instructions of the Holy Spirit as the Old Testament believers did. The parallel is drawn with a growing child who passes from total dependency in infancy to the mature adult able to stand on his own two feet. We can now stand on the full revelation of Scripture.

There is a mixture of truth and error here. Yes, God wants us to stand up and use our mature judgement rather than being told every little thing by the Holy Spirit. But no, biblical maturity is not equated with independence. A mature understanding sees that we are always dependent upon God. We can never outgrow that. Who was more mature than Jesus, the Son of God? Yet we see him moving in total dependence upon the Spirit of God: 'Jesus . . . was led by the Spirit' (Lk 4:1), and 'the Son can do nothing by himself' (Jn 5:19). If Jesus needed the guidance of the Holy Spirit, not only through the illumination of Scripture but in his direct 'leadings', then don't we? Would any of us want to say that we have matured to the point where we are beyond needing this guidance too? We are saying that Jesus needed it but we do not!

## Journey's end

I hope as we have travelled this long road together that you are all with me, firm converts to the truth that God speaks today. Having settled this, we can now address the question of how to receive this guidance.

*Part Two:*

*Reason*

# 4

# *Ways God Speaks*

By now we have hopefully established that God still speaks today—that he is still in the communication business in the twentieth century and has not retired from the scene, gracefully or otherwise. Now, what are we to look for from this great communicating God? Liver shivers? Audible voices? Chariots of fire? Writing on the wall? How *does* God speak? We also want to know what steps we need to take to hear his voice. Fasting and praying for forty days like Moses? Learning Freudian interpretations of dreams?

Not surprisingly, the Bible shows that God speaks in a great variety of ways. He is the God of variety in nature, and he is the God of variety in his dealings with man. Here are some of the ways God speaks.

## Audible voice

In 1 Samuel 3:4–14 we find God speaking in a voice that the boy Samuel could hear with his physical ears. It was so clear that it roused him from his bed, and it was so like a human voice that he mistook it for the chief priest, Eli. I do not know many people who frequently experience this type of guidance but I do know a girl who, while at university, was converted through hearing the Lord

just like Samuel did. She was lying alone on the grass
when she heard a voice call her name, 'Sarah.' (This is
not her real name.) She looked up to see who was calling
her, but there was no one around. She lay back down,
put it out of her mind, and, moments later, heard the
same voice. Somewhat anxiously this time, she again
glanced around to find that nobody was there! Again she
lay down, only to hear her name called a third time! She
finally figured out that it was the voice of God calling her.
She immediately went to find a church or a minister, and
she gave her heart to Jesus. God can speak with an
audible voice.

## Dreams

This is a common biblical way God speaks. God spoke to
Pharaoh in dreams which Joseph interpreted (Gen 41).
God spoke to Daniel in dreams (Dan 2:24ff; 4:19ff), as
well as enabling him to interpret others' dreams. God
spoke repeatedly to Joseph, Mary's husband, in dreams
(Mt 1:20; 2:13, 19, 22). So we should not be surprised if
God also wants to speak in this way to us.

## Visions

Rather than pictures coming to us while we are asleep as
in a dream, in visions pictures come to our conscious,
awake mind. The Bible is full of visions. The apostle Paul
started to evangelise Europe because of a vision (Acts
16:9). God's detailed unfolding of his programme for the
ages in the book of Revelation is mainly in the form of
visions. A whole book of visions!

However, visions are only one way God speaks. Thank
goodness for that. Visions are sometimes difficult to
understand. I recall one young man who, though not yet
converted, was seeking God and decided to read the
Bible, starting with the book of Revelation. His

conclusion was that the Bible was marvellously poetic, decidedly mystical, and, above all, difficult to comprehend. He wondered how he would ever get through the rest of the Bible if this one little book was taking him so long to work out. No, visions are not the only way or even the main way God speaks.

There are different sorts of visions. They range from the type that John had in the book of Revelation which were concrete and visible to the physical eye, to the more subjective type which are just pictures in the mind.

Yes, God can also speak by giving us pictures in our mind. A Youth With A Mission evangelism team was working with a tiny inner-city church seeking how they could effectively reach out to the local community. As they were praying God gave one of the team members a mental picture of the four of them singing and handing out tracts on the pavement directly outside the church entrance. The problem was that the church's location was definitely not a prime outreach spot. It was away from busy pedestrian traffic so that few people drifted past. Nevertheless, out they went on the basis of this guidance, and somebody wandered by who was desperate and looking for God. He came to the Lord on the spot. I have known outreaches in prime spots with many people listening where no one has come to the Lord. God is a good strategist.

## Angels

This is also a way God guides. God not only appears himself to guide, he also sends his angels as his representatives. 'Angel' in the Greek is actually the word 'messenger', and angels are God's celestial errand-boys. The splendour of these errand-boys is so magnificent that, should we catch a glimpse of them, we would be completely overwhelmed. Angels appeared to Abraham

(Gen 18), to Daniel (Dan 10:12), to Joseph (Mt 2:19), to Jesus (Mt 4:11), and to Peter (Acts 12:7).

An acquaintance of mine was going through a discouraging time in her work with a church in North London. During a prayer meeting she looked up across the room and saw an angel sitting on the bunk bed. She was struck by his radiance, not to mention the fact that he appeared to be about nine feet tall. He smiled, reassured her, and then, when she looked down, disappeared. Rest assured that when she told me this story I informed her that she had blown it. Had she been on her mettle, I suggested, she would have jumped in with all sorts of pertinent questions about cosmic travel, heaven and what it was like to live there. She certainly had no business just looking away in quiet awe. But it seems you rather lose presence of mind at a time like that.

Do you sometimes ask, 'Why doesn't that sort of thing ever happen to me?' That's what I often ask. The answer is that it is God's prerogative how he guides us. Our part is to be open and flexible so he can guide us in the way *he* wants, not necessarily in the way *we* want. When Peter inquired of the Lord about John's walk with God, Jesus replied, 'What is that to you? You must follow me' (Jn 21:22). In other words, 'How I deal with John isn't really your business. You just pay attention to the way I am leading you. You are not responsible for his life. You are responsible for *your* life.'

## Prophecies

The Bible is also a book full of God speaking through prophecies. Prophecy is both the foretelling of events before they happen and forth-telling—'telling forth' the mind of God on current events. It is still a gift in operation in the church today. That the 'gift of prophecy' mentioned in 1 Corinthians 12:10, 28 is not just hot preaching can be seen from other scriptures like 1 Corinthians 14:24–25 where prophecy is related to the secrets of someone's heart being revealed. It is something one could not know naturally. An example of this would be Peter knowing Ananias and Sapphira had lied in Acts 5. We see the prophet Agabus foretelling the future famine in Acts 11:27–28. He was a prophet, not a weather forecaster, so this was supernatural. We come upon Agabus in Acts 21:10–11 now foretelling the news that Paul would be bound by the Gentiles (one of those negative prophet types!). Agabus did not arrive at this conclusion as an astute political observer but as a prophet who could say, 'The Holy Spirit says. . .' It was revelation.

Now, while we embrace prophecy we need to see that another's prophecy over us, even with a 'thus saith the Lord' tacked on the end, does not necessarily constitute personal guidance for us. If God gives us guidance through another's prophecy, we need to wait on it until the Lord confirms it to us. The Lord is our shepherd, not that person.

The Bible says: 'Do not treat prophecies with contempt. Test everything. . .' (1 Thess 5:20–21). Receive prophecy, yet test it. Have a believing attitude but not a gullible one. Some of us are like a greedy diner who gulps down what is offered without taking proper time over it. Others of us are more like someone with an allergy. We gag when we hear a prophecy and automatically spit it out. When we hear a prophecy we need to strain it through a sieve and keep what is wholesome. We strain out the unwholesome bits by comparing a prophecy to the Scriptures and to what the Holy Spirit is saying to us.

We actually do not see in the New Testament someone's personal guidance coming through another's prophecy. In Acts 11:27–30 we see Agabus prophesying some events that were going to take place, but not what the believers should do about it. He did not give them directive guidance. In Acts 21:10–11 Agabus again only foretells the events which will take place in Jerusalem, not whether Paul should be going there or not. God had already told Paul that and given him his guidance (Acts 20:22–23). As a matter of fact the believers made a wrong conclusion on the basis of Agabus' prophecy of events and pleaded with him not to go (Acts 21:12). They were well meaning but wrong. Accepting prophecy is evidently only part of finding God's will and is no automatic guarantee that we are in God's will. Something similar was happening in Tyre where, 'Through the Spirit they urged Paul not to go on to Jerusalem' (Acts 21:4). It seems they were mixing what the Spirit was saying (ie, trouble) with what they were thinking (ie, avoid it). So we need to test prophecy.

In Acts 13:1–3 we have a case where prophecy probably did enter into someone's personal guidance. The prophets and church leaders were praying together when the Holy Spirit spoke to them (through prophecy?) about Paul and Barnabas' trip. Note that they had already been together on a one-year mission (Acts 11:26; 12:25) and undoubtedly already felt called together to this work anyway. The prophets just gave public recognition to what God was already saying.

While a reserve about accepting another's prophecy as directive guidance is altogether proper, one could not say that God never speaks through this means. In the Old Testament God often guided his people through the prophecy of others. And what he did in the past he can do in the present. Perhaps we do not see God guiding in this way in the New Testament because since Pentecost every believer possesses the Holy Spirit. God can speak directly to us and does not necessarily need to rely on a specially anointed messenger. But should God choose to speak to us through another, who are we to disagree?

## Witness of the Spirit

God witnesses to our spirit by his Spirit. This is not so much a compulsion or a voice as it is an inner assurance, conviction and peace. All Christians experience this. How do I know? In Romans 8:16 we read, 'The Spirit himself testifies with our spirit that we are God's children.' We know we are God's children through two means. The more objective assurance is God's promises as found in God's written word. He says if we repent and believe we will receive, and that's that. The more subjective assurance is the inner witness. 'We know that we know that we know.' As John says, 'And this is how we know that he lives in us: We know it by the Spirit he gave us' (1 Jn 3:24).

The point to notice here is that this 'witness' is quiet but *real*. If I were to ask some Christians whether or not the Holy Spirit ever communicated to them, they would say, 'Not that I know of.' However, he is testifying to their spirits right there and then, but because it is a quiet, subdued sort of communication they do not recognise it. It is not as though when we awake in the morning we stretch and then *it begins*! Our pulse quickens imperceptibly, our heart begins to pound, prickles run up the spine, a flush goes over our body as—*here it comes*—a little voice rises from deep within our hearts calling out, 'You're a Christian, you're a Christian, you're a Christian.' 'Boom, boom, boom,' goes our heart, and we are reassured for yet another day. The Spirit has just testified to our spirit. Hardly.

It has been said, 'Some Christians wouldn't recognise the Holy Spirit if he came walking down the street with a red hat on.' The reason we wouldn't is because he is more subtle than that. He gives a quiet conviction. It is this quiet conviction that is being referred to when Christians talk about 'feeling a peace'. We say we 'feel a peace' doing this or that. The often used proof-text for this phrase is Colossians 3:15: 'Let the peace of Christ rule in your hearts.' If the peace is ruling as you consider a subject then go ahead and do it. However, Colossians 3:15 refers not to guidance but to peace in our relationships. And while Romans 8:6—'the mind controlled by the Spirit is life and peace'—may relate to guidance, it more properly refers to the wider truth of our peace with God, with ourselves and with our neighbours.

In the end, it is unimportant whether the phrase 'feel a peace' originates from Colossians 3:16 or Romans 8:6. What is important is not the phrase but the reality of the experience it describes. 'Feeling a peace' could just be another way of describing the witness of the Spirit of Romans 8:16. This witness takes the form of a conviction and an assurance within us, which is just another way of saying it produces a peace.

This 'witness of the Spirit' played a large part in my choice of a marriage partner. Not only did the natural factors add up (she was beautiful and I was perceptive!) but I had a deep witness in my spirit that she was the right girl. I never saw any visions, heard an audible voice or had a scripture burned into my soul. I just knew it was right. Now I just had to convince her of it!

This 'witness' can seem like a 'prod' from the Spirit. I recall being in Kabul, Afghanistan, in the early 1970s where I was part of a ministry to Western travellers who came searching for an exotic mixture of drugs, adventure and religion. I was on the way to one of our downtown ministry centres when I noticed a long-haired young man stepping out of a bicycle taxi. I walked by trying to shake off the feeling that I should have a word with him. The further I got away from the taxi the stronger the compulsion grew to go back to speak with him. For my own peace of mind, I went back to him, struck up a conversation, and to my delight found that he was a non-Christian interested in Jesus who had been wandering around the city specifically looking for our ministry centre! With my usual spiritual sensitivity and insight, I concluded that God had guided me to this fellow. The 'prod of the Spirit' may not be a biblical term but it is a biblical reality. God urges us, almost compels us at times.

This does not mean that God wants us to be compulsive people continually following our whims and feelings. This will not make us spiritual, just neurotic! We need to ask God to teach us to discern the difference between our feelings and the Holy Spirit's compulsions. Our protection against a neurotic compulsiveness is to realise that God guides us through our understanding (see Chapter 4) and that God will clearly confirm his will. He does not expect us to act on vague and hazy impressions.

## Still, small voice

Not only can God give us a compulsion and a drive to do something, not only can he guide us through a witness of the Spirit, God can also guide us by actually speaking a thought into our mind. Rather than an intuitive 'sense'— which is the essence of our previous two forms of guidance—the still small voice communicates a clear thought. 'Do this. Don't do that. Go here.'

The famous scripture referring to God speaking in a still, small voice is 1 Kings 19:11–13. The Lord was going to appear to Elijah and speak to him. How would he do it? Would he come to Elijah with a spectacular display full of sound and fury? No, he did not appear and speak through the ripping wind, nor through the ear-splitting earthquake, nor through the raging fire. He spoke in a gentle whisper. God does not always speak in a spectacular way. Heart palpitations, liver shivers, and tingles up the spine (the inner equivalents of hurricane winds, earthquakes, and fire) do not always accompany his voice. They do sometimes, but often God will just speak in a still, small voice.

That is why it is easy to miss. 'That's just me', we say.

There are times when that idea we are dismissing as 'just my own thought' is God communicating to us. It is our own thought but *it has been put there by God*! In other words, God's thoughts in our mind do not have a special spiritual vibration or spooky 'other-worldly' feel about them which differentiate them from our own thoughts. They feel and sound just like our own thoughts because they *are* our own thoughts . . . only they have been put there by God.

We can see how natural God's voice is when we remember little Samuel who twice mistook God's voice for his master Eli's voice. God's voice sounded like a human voice in this case. It was not an exceptionally deep bass voice, nor did it have a peculiar quaver: 'Saaa-muelllll.' If it had been a spooky and other-wordly voice Samuel would not have mistook it. If his audible voice can be so unspectacular, how much less surprising that his still, small inner voice is unspectacular.

We learn to tell the difference between our thoughts and God's thoughts through experience. Doing it, doing it, doing it, is the key to learning in every area of our Christian lives. But we need more than experience. We need a teachable attitude where we try to learn from our experience. As they say in management circles, on-the-job training is more than just showing up at work. Pay attention and be teachable.

We grow in sensitivity as we pray, listen and step out. Hebrews 5:14 says, 'But solid food is for the mature, who by constant use have trained themselves to distinguish good from evil.' The writer is saying that our sensitivity to good and evil is developed by constant use of our conscience. So it is with our spiritual sensitivity to the Lord's voice. It is developed as we use it. Perhaps the Lord has been speaking to us a lot more than we think, but we just have not known it was him as we were waiting for a heavenly thunderclap and a quavery voice saying, 'This is the Loorrddd!'

Consider the following story, evidently true:

An American Indian was in downtown New York with his friend, who lived in New York City. Suddenly he said, 'I hear a cricket.'

'Oh, you're crazy,' his friend replied.

'No, I hear a cricket. I do! I'm sure of it.'

'It's the noon hour. There are people bustling around, cars honking, taxis squealing, noises from the city. I'm sure you can't hear it.'

'I'm sure I do.' He listened attentively, crossed the street to the opposite corner and looked all around. Finally he spotted a shrub in a large cement planter. He dug beneath the leaves and found a cricket.

His friend was astounded. But the Cherokee said, 'No. My ears are no different from yours. It simply depends on what you are listening to. Here, let me show you.'

He reached into his pocket and pulled out a handful of change—a few quarters, some dimes, nickels and pennies. And he dropped it on the concrete. Every head within a block turned.

'You see what I mean?' he said as he began picking up his coins. 'It all depends on what you are listening for.'[6]

God speaks and we can hear his voice. He not only will speak to us directly about situations, but he will also speak a scripture reference into our mind. Let me relate some of my personal experiences, not because they are especially glorious but because they are what I know best.

One summer, thirty to forty volunteers were coming to London to evangelise with a Youth With A Mission 'Summer of Service' (SOS) team that I was leading. Shortly before they were to arrive I learned that our mission was having an important conference in Thailand the same week the SOS started. I thought I should probably be attending the conference, but as I considered my responsibilities for the SOS I thought, 'This is crazy to leave for that first important week. What will the summer participants think of my leadership?' So as I waited before the Lord the scripture reference Mark 3:21 popped into my mind. Looking it up I found that it read as follows: 'When his family heard about this, they went to take charge of him, for they said, "He is out of his mind." ' I thought, 'Well, if it was okay for Jesus, it's okay for me.' Off I went to the Thailand conference assured by the Lord that it might seem crazy but it was his will.

On another occasion I became friendly with somebody in a builders' merchants who later that day phoned me up asking for money. He needed £30 to get him to Finland so that he could start the job waiting for him there. What to do? As Christians we want to be generous, but we also want to be good stewards of God's money and give it where he wants. I told the man to phone me back in fifteen minutes. Meanwhile I waited on the Lord who spoke the scripture 1 Timothy 6:5 into my mind. I looked it up and read, '. . . who think that godliness is a means to financial gain.' I took it to mean God did not want me to give the money. This man probably just took me for a Christian 'soft touch'. With great peace I turned down the man's request. The more we talked on the phone the more his insincerity became evident. And so I felt confirmed in what I felt the Lord had said.

As a final illustration, let me cite the time I was asking God for confirmation that the vision some friends and I had of beginning a music band was really his vision. We had just started a band called *The Survivors*, of which I was the mixer-manager. (Some thought 'mixed-up manager' was a more fitting description!) As I waited on the Lord he spoke into my mind, 'I have already told you.'

'You have?' I thought. 'Where?'

'What was that foundational scripture you were given years ago? Well look at it,' God replied.

Some four years earlier when we had first moved to London, a friend gave my wife and I a scripture which she believed was God's word for us. It was Isaiah 37:30–31. It spoke of a kind of spiritual sequence in the first, second and third year (and indeed the 'Summer of Service' in our third year had been especially fruitful). So, I looked at it and said, 'Yes Lord, but what does this have to do with my question about the band?'

'Keep reading,' came back the thought.

It was then that I came across something I had never noticed before. Verse 32 states, 'For out of Jerusalem will come a remnant, and out of Mount Zion a *band of survivors* (italics mine).'

'Thank you, Lord,' I said. 'I think we are on the right track.'

## No fuzzy impressions, please

Before we leave this subject of God's still, small voice, there is one more issue that we need to address. Some Christians would question the reality of this 'still, small voice'. They would say that we do not see this quiet, difficult to discern, inner voice in Scripture. Inner impressions posing as the 'still, small voice' are dismissed as the emotional 'voice' of the person himself. They would point out that when God spoke to people in the Scriptures it was in a very clear and definitely supernatural way. No fuzzy, subjective impressions here! For instance, there was no mistaking God's voice for a human voice in the calling of Moses back to Egypt (Ex 3). It came complete with a mysteriously burning bush. This was God! Samuel, too, heard a loud, clear voice and not an inner voice (1 Sam 3). God spoke in a literally thunderous voice to Jesus (Jn 12:29). No subtlety there! God's voice at Saul's conversion came over in a technicolour extravaganza (Acts 9:3ff). All of these people knew it was God who was speaking, and there was no question about it.

My response to this is twofold. Firstly, there are many cases of God communicating clearly, spectacularly and unmistakably. There are also cases of ambiguous, subtle

and hidden divine communication. The same voice that
spoke with thunderous clarity to Jesus was mistaken by
others as a mere thunderclap (Jn 12:29). When two angels
and the Lord appeared to Abraham on their way to
Sodom, Abraham mistook them for men at first, and
offered them hospitality (Gen 18). This was not at first
an obvious divine encounter. Of course, the whole incar-
nation and life of Jesus is the story of God communicating
his divine treasure through an ordinary, unspectacular
human-looking vessel. That is why so many people missed
seeing who Jesus was. Look at the way Jesus reveals the
historic, world-changing event that was the resurrection.
He is so low-key, subtle and unspectacular that his own
disciples do not recognise him. The two disciples on the
Emmaus road just took him to be an uninformed traveller
(Lk 24:15ff). Mary mistook him for an ordinary gardener
(Jn 20:15). The twelve mistook him for just another
fisherman or man on the beach (Jn 21:4ff). God first
communicated to the patriarch Jacob in a dream (Gen
28:12). At first this seems a fairly spectacular form of
communication until you think how easy it would have
been to dismiss it as simply the result of too much late-
night pizza. (I will grant that this was a harder excuse to
'swallow' in pre-Pizza Hut Canaan.) So it is not true that
his communications are always obviously supernatural.

We have not proved the reality of subjective
impressions simply by establishing the fact that God's
guidance can be subtle. His first approach to the boy
Samuel was subtle but it was still audible. This brings us
to the next point.

Secondly, the Scriptures give multiple examples of guidance that had to be of the subjective 'still, small voice'
variety. No other explanation adequately explains the
scriptures in question. Here are a few.

Luke 2:27: 'Moved by the Spirit, he went into the
temple courts.' The impression is not given that Simeon
heard an audible, spectacular voice. He either heard

God's inner voice, felt a compulsion to go, or was being led unconsciously by the Lord.

Luke 2:28-32: 'Simeon took him (Jesus) in his arms and praised God, saying, ". . . my eyes have seen your salvation. . . ." ' How did he know this? God obviously spoke to him there on the spot. The question here is *how* did God speak and reveal it to Simeon. There was no audible voice and no spectacular flashing lights. God obviously just spoke in his heart saying something to the effect of, 'This is the Saviour you have been waiting for.' The point is that it was an inner, subjective revelation. It was subtle but definitely of God.

Luke 1:41-45. Here we see Elizabeth receiving communication from God and prophesying over Mary. How did God communicate with her? Again there is no indication of an outer, objective, tangible supernatural manifestation. The reason she knew is because she 'was filled with the Holy Spirit' (v. 41). The Holy Spirit spoke to her spirit. It was an inner, subjective experience. She just knew.

Luke 1:67. Here is Zechariah prophesying over his son, John the Baptist. All that we said about Elizabeth applies to Zechariah. We should not be surprised that the Holy Spirit speaks in this inner way. Look at this next scripture.

1 Peter 1:10-11: '. . . the prophets, who spoke of . . . circumstances to which the Spirit of Christ in them was pointing when he predicted. . . .' Here is the prophetic pattern. It was the Holy Spirit within them that communicated. It was an inner voice. The prophets did not hear a booming voice in the sky dictating words which they then furiously copied in shorthand. No, the Spirit within them spoke. They spoke from the burdens God had put on their hearts.

2 Peter 1:21: 'For prophecy never had its origin in the will of man, but men spoke from God as they were carried along by the Holy Spirit.' That is an interesting phrase:

'carried along'. God is not just speaking out there but within us.

John 5:19, 30: '. . . the Son can do nothing by himself; he can do only what he sees his Father doing . . . I judge only as I hear. . . .' If we take this scripture at face value it can only mean that Jesus did not do things by his own strength or according to his own intelligence. He looked to his Father in heaven. He was supernaturally led. He followed where he saw God at work, and he made decisions as he heard from God. How did this supernatural leading come to Jesus? Objective, audible voices, or subjective impressions? Are the Gospels full of recorded incidents of God's audible voice leading Jesus? No! The twelve apostles were constantly around Jesus, and they would have had ample opportunity to observe and record these divine meetings. They did when they saw them. The gospel writers record only a few instances of the more spectacular kinds of guidance. Evidently, the supernatural leadings Jesus 'saw' and 'heard' were of a quiet and inner sort. Quiet, unremarkable, but very real.

How did Jesus know that Nathaniel was under a fig-tree (Jn 1:50)? Philip did not record something as spectacular as a booming, heavenly voice. No, Jesus heard God's voice with his 'inner' ear. It was the same still, small voice of God which speaks to us today.

We have spent a good deal of space and print on guidance through the still, small voice because it seems to have occupied a key place in the New Testament records. We need to understand it and reach out for it if we are to transfer it from being a New Testament, apostolic experience to a twentieth century 'me' experience.

Of course, there are dangers to this kind of teaching. People could and have 'felt led' to do all sorts of crazy and God-dishonouring things. But there are dangers to all forms of guidance. On the grounds of faithfulness to the Scriptures Christians have burned heretics, drowned

Anabaptists and enslaved blacks. We do need protections, and we shall look at some later in this chapter.

## Daily reading of Scripture

God can speak to some specific question we are asking him out of our regular reading of the Bible. Psalm 119:105 says, 'Your word is a lamp to my feet and a light for my path.' When finding your way along a dark path at night, it is silly to only periodically get your lamp out. We need to continually hold the lamp before us, so we need to continuously read our Bibles. It is then that the Holy Spirit can speak from his word and especially impress some truth on us.

## The Random Access Bible

The Bible has its own RAM (random access memory), as does a computer. This method is to pray God will lead you, open the Scriptures at random, plonk your finger down anywhere, and then see what you have caught. But watch out. Some people have caught a man-eating shark! There is the story of someone trying this method three times only to come up first with, 'Judas . . . went away and hanged himself' (Mt 27:5), and then, 'Go and do likewise' (Lk 10:37), followed finally by, 'What you are about to do, do quickly' (Jn 13:27). There is also the story of a Christian sitting out a V2 rocket attack on London during World War II. Seeking comfort she reached into her promise box filled with scripture cards only to pull out Habakkuk 2:3: '. . . though it tarry, wait for it; because it will surely come, it will not tarry' (KJV).

John Wesley's experience with this method demonstrates both the dangers and possible usefulness of this method. In 1739 the eloquent George Whitefield pleaded with Wesley to replace him at Bristol. Whitefield was preaching with much effect to crowds of up to 10,000 in the open air, but he felt he should be going on to America. Four times Wesley 'consulted the oracle' (opened his Bible at random), and each time the verse he lighted upon referred to death or suffering. Sure that he would die, Wesley refused to go. Keeping up this method he hit a verse telling him to go anyway, which he dutifully obeyed. With this he was launched into his nation-shaking ministry. The death he feared did not come upon him. He lived into his eighties! This method of guidance got him going, but only after some bumps and starts.[7]

I do not recommend this method because Scripture holds out the promise that we can hear his voice. This method does not seem to latch onto this promise, but smacks more of a desperate, last-ditch effort to find God's will in a haphazard way. The Scripture also indicates that God will use our mind in guidance, and this method completely ignores our God-given judgement.

Despite these reservations, there is some New Testament precedent for its use. It is the equivalent of 'the drawing of lots', or drawing the shortest straw. The apostles used this drawing lots method to find God's will between two suitable candidates for apostleship (Acts 1:21–26). Please notice that it was their God-given and biblically informed reason which was the original basis for choosing these two men. Only afterwards did they use lots. Drawing lots finds a place in Scripture, but only a minor one. So should it be with the 'random access Bible' method.

### Circumstances

God can also speak to us through the circumstances he brings or allows. Saul's son, Jonathan, was itching to get out and vindicate God's name against a Philistine nation that had no respect for Israel and even less respect for their God. What should he do? What would God's will be for him? He decided to take a step, and if God opened up the circumstances before him he would take that as confirmation that it was God's will to proceed. God did just that, and a mighty victory was won for Israel (1 Sam 14:6–15).

The famous 'Gideon's fleece' of Judges 6 falls into this department. It was a confirming circumstance which brought certainty to Gideon that what he thought was the will of God was just that. My motto on fleeces is: 'Beware of fleecing God, for the devil may fleece you.' Translated that means that we should not press God for all sorts of weird and wonderful events to occur before we believe God is leading us. 'If that's you God, let it rain frogs tomorrow.' Don't wait for this kind of confirmation because they are probably not on the heavenly forecast.

Why should the Christian not use far-fetched, unusual circumstances of the 'If you want me to go, Lord, then have my pastor walk in with a purple tie with yellow splashes on it' variety? Firstly, because it usually arises out of unbelief rather than faith. Without faith we cannot please God. We do not trust that we can really hear from God so we resort to concrete, visible signs. We feel more comfortable with the concrete, just as pagans of old felt more comfortable with concrete idols than with an invisible God. Secondly, it is wrong because it is looking to outward signs rather than to the Holy Spirit within us. The Holy Spirit has come to dwell within our hearts and he means to be our counsellor. He wants to lead us. To look without us is not exactly the equivalent of spitting in his face, but it is a failure to rely on the Holy Spirit's ability to communicate to us.

While God does not want us to look to silly circumstances as our prime source of guidance, he will use outside situations to show us his will. An acquaintance of mine was confused about his sense of humour which he displayed in leading a church youth group. Someone accused him of being frivolous, so naturally he began to question the godliness of his sense of humour. Was this

condemnation of the devil or conviction from the Holy
Spirit? He sought God. One day a lad who did not know
any of his struggles approached him. He told my friend,
'You know, before I came to this youth group I didn't
like Christians because I thought to be a Christian was to
be stuffy. But you are one of the liveliest, "jokiest"
people around. And that has really helped me to change
my way of thinking. So I have now given my life to Christ.
Thanks!' Well my friend had got his answer from God
about his humour, and God had done it through a life
situation rather than through something 'supernatural'
like a vision.

God not only wants us to hear his voice and learn from
the Bible, but also to learn from the life situations he
brings our way. 'What is God trying to teach me in this
situation?' is a question we should be asking God. Proverbs
6:6 says, 'Go to the ant, you sluggard; consider its ways and
be wise!' Bird watchers we know about, but it seems that
the Bible tells us more about ant watchers. Life is a storehouse of wisdom for those who will learn from it.

## Steps to hearing God's voice

We have seen the ways God speaks. Our next question
is how do we get into the place of hearing his voice, of
receiving his guidance? If God gives guidance but we
cannot hear it then we are still not helped. There's God's
part (speaking), and our part (listening). How do we go
about doing our part? My seven suggested steps are:
1. Confess known sin.
2. Submit to God.
3. Be dependent.
4. Resist the devil.
5. Expect an answer.
6. Wait on God.
7. Ask for confirmation.
Let me look at each step in detail.

### 1. Confess known sin

Psalm 66:18: 'If I had cherished sin in my heart, the Lord would not have listened.' What is the point of asking to know more of God's will if we are not obeying what he has already shown us to do? God does not reveal his will for us to peruse through it and speculate upon it, but that we might obey it. So we must get any past disobedience straightened out by confession and repentance.

### 2. Submit to God

Not only do we need to straighten out the past, we need to submit our present to the Lord. We want to have the attitude of Jesus when he said, 'Yet not my will, but yours be done' (Lk 22:42). This attitude is key in finding God's will. Jesus also said, 'If anyone chooses to do God's will, he will find out whether my teaching comes from God. . .' (Jn 7:17). Understanding starts with a heart attitude of submission to do God's will. It would be pointless of God to reveal his will to any except those who want to obey.

### 3. Be dependent

Proverbs 3:5: 'Trust in the Lord with all your heart and lean not on your own understanding.' Jeremiah 10:23: 'I know, O Lord, that a man's life is not his own; it is not for man to direct his steps.' This realisation is one that God works into us through the hard knocks of life. But it is also an attitude we can choose. We choose to look to God and ask for his help. Being dependent is more than a specific step in guidance, but is an underlying attitude that will motivate us to seek guidance in the first place.

Independence would say, 'I've done this before. I know the scriptures on this issue. God has taught me lessons on this in the past. I can handle it on my own now.' Dependence would say, 'Despite the wisdom and experience you have given me in this area, I still need you,

Lord, to give me fresh insight, power and anointing.' If we are independent we will depend on our own wisdom and experience rather than looking to the Lord for his fresh guidance. Then it will be a case of, '. . . ye have not, because ye ask not' (Jas 4:2, KJV).

Man is a dependent animal. Physically he needs food. Emotionally he needs love. Every which way he needs God. I am writing this chapter at my brother-in-law's house in northern Michigan, situated in beautiful, wooded country. Going for a drive on my first day there, we crested a hill, whereupon I was regaled with the sight of a spectacularly blue lake set like a glistening sapphire in a ring of trees that covered the valley. Glorious! The following day we went for another drive. Climbing the same hill I eagerly anticipated another breathtaking glimpse of my jewel in the woods. But what a let-down to crest the hill only to be presented with a drab, dishwater grey lake. What had happened to my lake? The lake was the same, the trees were the same, but the sun was hidden by clouds. The sky being dull and colourless meant that the lake would be dull and colourless. The lake's beauty was a reflected beauty—and so is ours. Our wisdom, too, is a reflected wisdom. We are dependent on God for it. The more we realise that the better.

## 4. Resist the devil

James 4:7: 'Submit yourselves, then, to God. Resist the devil, and he will flee from you.' There are three possible voices in our mind: God's voice, our own voice, or the devil's voice. Our goal is to hear God's voice and not to mistake it for our voice or the devil's. How do we keep the devil's voice out? By resisting him, James says. Resisting the devil consists of not succumbing to his temptation (we then resist his will) and silencing his voice by commanding him to be silent 'in the name of Jesus'. Use your authority as a believer.

Do what Jesus did when Satan spoke to him. He said, 'Away from me, Satan!' The result? 'Then the devil left him. . .' (Mt 4:10–11). This is the same result we will have when *we* command the devil. James promised that, 'He will flee from you.' Why does he flee? It is because Jesus defeated him at the cross, and we Christians share in that victory. The devil knows he is defeated (Mt 8:29; Rev 12:12); do Christians?

If the Scriptures show anything, they show that the devil is talkative. He talked Eve into sin in the garden of Eden. He talked to Jesus on the mountain, trying to tempt him into sin. And he even dares to talk to God, to accuse us to him (Rev 12:10)! Let's take this talkative, lying ministry into account when we seek guidance. Talk back to him. Bind his voice and command him to be still in Jesus' name.

## 5. *Expect an answer*

Hebrews 11:6: 'And without faith it is impossible to please God, because anyone who comes to him must believe that he exists and that he rewards those who earnestly seek him.' The writer says we 'must believe'. After all, what is the point of asking God a question if we do not expect an answer. We might as well not pray in that case.

Faith is not a mysterious 'something' we need to be zapped with. Faith is simply believing that God will do what he said in his word of promise that he would do. What did he say he would do? 'He will guide you . . . he will speak. . .' (Jn 16:13). My Greek is a bit rusty, but I suspect the word 'speak' in the 1st Century carried the same connotation as 'speak' does in the 20th Century. It means communication of the verbal sort. No subtleties there. *He will speak.*

Expectant faith is key to every area of the Christian walk. God is not absolutely prevented from speaking or acting by our unbelief, but he certainly is hindered. Our expectancy is extinguished by a theology which says that

Holy Spirit guidance was only for apostolic times. If this theology drowns expectancy, then it is at least dampened by the teaching that though supernatural guidance is possible, it is extremely rare. As one book on guidance put it, 'Most of us will *never* (my emphasis) experience supernatural guidance.' These are strong words. I do not see the Scriptures saying that.

Jesus promised, 'My sheep hear My voice . . . he calls his own sheep by name, and leads them out' (Jn 10:27, 3, NASB). Let me make several observations from this verse.

(a) As stated in Chapter 2, the voice referred to here is God's spoken word, spoken by the Spirit and not just in God's written word, the Bible. It says, 'He calls his own sheep by name', and there are many names that are not written in the Bible. So this verse must be referring to his Spirit's voice.

(b) It is a promise to all his sheep and not just to the super-spiritual, extra-sensitive sheep. If you can say 'Baaa', you qualify. All Christians cash in on this promise. Not only do the Bible 'greats' hear God's voice, but ordinary men and women like Ananias (Acts 9:10) and the shepherds outside Bethlehem (Lk 2:8ff).

(c) There is a difference between 'hearing' (v 3) and 'knowing' (v 4) his voice. To hear is to receive the sounds without necessarily recognising the source. To know is to hear the voice plus recognise it. The difference is illustrated every day on the telephone. When you are rung by a stranger you tend to answer in flat, polite, neutral tones. But should a good friend phone, your voice rises in excitement, 'Well, hellooo!' You know that voice. It registers. You have not only heard, you have recognised his voice.

That we 'hear' his voice is a description of present reality. That we 'know' his voice is often more a promise of future reality. It is a promised inheritance we need to fight for even as the Israelites fought for their promised land of Caanaan. The Bible says we do 'hear' God's voice, but sometimes we do not 'know' it and recognise it. Sheep are dumb, but that's okay because they know their master's voice. We Christians can be smarter than sheep, but worse off in that we do not know the Master's voice. We will grow in familiarity with his voice as we listen to it and act on it.

(d) Our confidence in hearing from God is based on the fact that God works on both the sending and receiving end. The picture is not of God sending out signals from his power station in heaven only to have it all go awry because we have been unable to fine-tune our receiver sufficiently. This verse says we do 'hear', so God must be insuring that our hearing faculties are well serviced and doing the job. Do not be discouraged by the thought that you are not spiritually sensitive enough to hear God's voice. The word says, 'My sheep hear my voice'. That's you! That's a promise!

We can expect God to guide us and speak to us on the basis of these clear promises of Scripture. Jesus said, 'According to your faith will it be done to you' (Mt 9:29). As it is in healing, so it is with guidance. 'Blessed are those who expect nothing for they shall not be disappointed!' Decide to believe in your heart that God will answer your quest for guidance.

In believing that God can speak to us we are flying in the face of the western worldview in which we have been raised. Our western world believes in a mechanistic, impersonal universe. Abstract laws dominate, and there is no room for a personal God who intervenes. Science is the ultimate reality, and everything else is seen as superstition. A belief in miracles and guidance is seen as a reversion to the Dark Ages long ago outgrown by sophisticated, modern man. Those of us who have grown up in the western world have not escaped the influence of this worldview. In the back of our mind lies a nagging doubt whispering, 'You're crazy. Hearing voices now, are you?

Next it will be pink elephants!'

Don't be thrown. Remember that even belief in science is a faith. You cannot get away from faith. The question is, which is more reasonable: to trust in man or to trust in God? Have the courage of your convictions and follow them through to their end consequences. If there is a living God then it comes as no surprise that he can speak.

Expect God to speak. And remember to let him speak to you in his way and time. Do not dictate to God. He is the boss! You may be wanting a scripture, and he may want to give you a 'witness of the Spirit' or a picture. You may want to know now, but it may be necessary to seek the Lord a second time the next day.

## 6. Give God the chance to speak

Wait on him in silence, listening. Do not just spend twenty minutes unloading your burdens and asking God questions without also waiting for the answers. Wouldn't you feel puzzled if someone treated you that way? After all, that is why we are asking the questions, isn't it? Is it? Do not just plead, 'Guide me, guide me,' without giving God time to give this earnestly sought guidance. Otherwise, we may rush out of our prayer closets just as God is about to speak. He might have been waiting for us to finish speaking so he could speak, only to find that we have rushed off once we have concluded our monologue.

Prayer is an excellent way to get something 'off our chest', but it is more than that. It is also a way God can get something 'off *his* chest' and into our hearts. And it is God's provision for two-way communication where not only does God get to listen to us, but we can listen to God. Have you ever tried to listen carefully to somebody while you talked to them at the same time? It is difficult. Really, you can only do one or the other. It is the same with God. We need to be both asking and listening.

'Be still, and know that I am God' (Ps 46:10). '. . . Some of the elders of Israel came to enquire of the Lord, and they sat down in front of me' (Ezek 20:1). Sit still before God. Have you ever tried talking to someone as they are running out the door? It's frustrating! It is better to have them sitting down in front of us giving us their undivided attention. In Exodus 24:16, we see Moses waiting six days on Mount Sinai till God spoke to him. There is a quite literal meaning to the biblical phrase 'waiting on God', and Moses was practising it. It means waiting. Not too deep, but there it is. Jesus prayed all through the night before he chose his twelve apostles (Lk 6:12–13). He gave God his Father time to speak to him.

Unbelief (besides not wanting to know God's will) is the main reason we do not wait on him in prayer. Frankly, we are just not convinced that this waiting will accomplish anything. If it goes on for any extended time, it can seem a bit of a waste of time. The underlying reason for these feelings is we doubt that at the end of our time of waiting we will come up with something from God. We fear it will be in vain.

We are willing to wait an hour to see the doctor, or several hours to see a civil servant because we know that eventually we will get in to see the desired person. We are not so convinced, however, with God. We are afraid he will leave us to rot in the waiting room. Or perhaps we fear that there is no one beyond the waiting room who will really speak to us. But, good news, God is more faithful than even the most devoted civil servant. He will make good his promise that 'he will speak' (Jn 16:13).

Waiting on God in silence is a concrete way to give expression to the faith we have that God speaks. '. . . Faith by itself, if it is not accompanied by action, is dead . . . his faith and his actions were working together, and his faith was made complete by what he did' (Jas 2:17, 22). Faith needs expression. If we believe God speaks we will spend time listening, both to his written word and to his Spirit.

Do not be upset by the fact that you find you have a wandering mind and a short attention span. He knows what we are like and is not shocked and disturbed by it. He can still speak to us despite all that. Just continue seeking him, perhaps punctuating your periods of silence with periods of reading and quoting scriptures, singing praises, or intercessions. This will help to keep your mind focused on God.

## 7. Ask God for confirmation

If you think God has guided and spoken to you on a certain point, do not be afraid to ask for confirmation. It need not be an expression of unbelief. Rather, it is wisdom. It is simply recognition that we could have been mistaken in hearing God.

'Test everything,' the scripture commands (1 Thess 5:21). Far from recommending gullibility, the scriptures speak disapprovingly of the 'simple man (who) believes anything' (Prov 14:15). God wants us to check impressions and leadings to see if they are from God, both our own impressions and the words of others for us. Rather than being intimidated by someone's 'thus saith the Lord' and pressurised into the course of action they are recommending, take it to the Lord for confirmation.

The more important a decision is, the more we need confirmation. God wants instant obedience. But God does not want rash or impulsive Christians who run off down some exotic path at the very first hint of a leading. Responsible stewardship is a Christian principle. Not only are we to be good stewards of our time and money, but of our life directions. Good stewards are not rash. God wants us to make prayed through, thought out decisions.

See how patiently and willingly God gave Moses repeated confirmations to go back to Egypt in Exodus 3–4. It was a major change of direction to go from tending sheep to delivering Israelites. Imagine contemplating confronting the most powerful world ruler of the day on his own turf with your only visible weapon being a knobbly staff! Moses needed confirmation! And God gave it to him. God will. God only became angry with Moses (Ex 4:14) when in the face of clear, recurrent confirmation, Moses backed out in unbelief. Even when Moses was sure it was God speaking, he still would not accept his call. This is what displeased the Lord. God is not at all displeased with our endeavour to insure we are hearing from him by looking for confirmation. Let us be sure to believe and follow his direction once he has made it clear.

Pastor Charles Blair, in his book *The Man Who Could Do No Wrong*, tells the story of how he, a successful pastor of a 5,000-member American church, took on the task of building a hospital for God. He had the best intentions and felt he had God's leading, but the end result was failure, public humiliation and involvement in fraud. What went wrong? Looking back, pastor Blair writes that he was not careful enough in seeking proper confirmation; he made the mistake of having faith in faith, of trying to 'believe' his way through every difficulty rather than rechecking his fundamental direction. He thought caution was a sign of unbelief. It isn't. Seek confirmation.

Here are some of the things we look for as confirmation:

*1. Biblical principles.* We need to firstly check that our guidance fits within biblical morality. God will not contradict his word.

*2. Counsellors.* 'Plans fail for lack of counsel, but with many advisers they succeed' (Prov 15:22). Christianity is not a lifestyle of 'just me and Jesus'. God gives us protection and wisdom indirectly through people as well as directly from heaven. We need a good balance between a dynamic faith in God's ability to speak to us and a heavenly humility which recognises that God speaks to and through others. God keeps us humble by having us depend on weak, fallible people and not just on a mighty

God.

Of course, we have to weigh up the advice of our counsellors. We need not automatically accept it. However, as we listen to their advice with an open mind we can trust that God will give us the wisdom to weigh their advice properly.

*3. More words.* Moses asked God questions and wanted to hear more from God before proceeding. There is no reason to leap off at the first vague leading or scriptural impression. We can ask God to give us more leadings and scriptures.

*4. Prophecy.* We have already seen how in Acts 21:11 prophecies functioned not as original guidance, but as confirmation to Paul.

*5. Circumstances.* God used a circumstantial sign to reveal the right bride for Isaac (Gen 24:14). Favourable circumstances giving opportunities for effective service were what convinced Paul to stay on in Ephesus (1 Cor 16:8–9). Circumstances can be a final confirmation that a certain course is God's will. Of course, a mountain in our path is no guaranteed sign that God does not want us going down that road. We may have to climb over the mountain or move it with the command of faith. Circumstances are not an absolute indicator of God's will, but they are one of the confirmations he uses.

*6. Common sense.* It is quite scriptural to weigh up rationally our guidance. Common sense is not an absolute guide, but it is part of being made in the image of God. We shall investigate its function more in Chapters 4 and 5.

### What if God is silent?

What do you do when you pray and wait on the Lord and no answer seems to come from heaven? Here are some suggestions:

*1. Maintain trust.* Do not get frustrated. Easily said, I know. This may sound as helpful as saying, 'Don't worry,' to a chronic stress patient. Nevertheless, we can choose to trust.

We panic over guidance when we begin to fret over whether God will really get his guidance through to us. Then Satan gets in on the act and compounds the problem with his lies. 'You don't really know God or his voice,' he will whisper. Satan winds us up. Trust winds us down.

2. *Continue to pray and wait.* We have seen how Moses prayed for days (Ex 24:15–16), how Jesus prayed all night (Lk 6:12), and how Daniel prayed continuously for three weeks before his answer came through (Dan 10:12, 14). Some things just take time. One thing an eternal God has is time. So learn to persevere in waiting.

3. *Consider whether God wants to guide us in another way.* It may be that God is not going to give us a definite answer in prayer. We may need to just go ahead and make a decision. We will discuss this further in the following chapters.

## God is not hibernating

God still speaks. He has not gone into a hibernation of wintry silence after a brief bout of activity in some golden apostolic age, only to emerge with a shout at his second coming. 'In those days the word of the Lord was rare' (1 Sam 3:1) described an Israel whose spiritual vitality was at low ebb. It was never meant to be a satisfactory description of our age when 'The kingdom of God is near' (Mk 1:15). Don't allow it to be the pronouncement that rings out over your life.

# 5

# *Reason's Place in Walking with God*

## Failing to plan is planning to fail

The other day a young couple walked into my room and
started up a conversation that went something like this:
'My husband and I struggle because we have a completely
different way of going about making decisions. I guess I
am just not up to his level of faith. He goes on a word
from the Lord, but I tend to use my reason. For instance,
the other week a ministry opportunity came our way in
another part of the country and we needed to know
whether we should take it. After we had prayed about it
we felt that the Lord probably wanted us to go. The
problem was that only half the team had the necessary
finances. Still, my husband felt that because we had
prayed about it we ought to go and trust that the money
would all come in. I thought we should make a contingency plan in case the money did not come in. He said
that would be acting in unbelief, an exercise in negative
faith. He said that would be a guaranteed way to block
up the provision of the needed money according to the
principle, "According to your faith will it be done to you"
(Mt 9:29). I guess I am just not up to his standard of
faith. Well, the money never did come in. We waited till
the last minute for the finances and then in a flurry had

to cancel the trip. Because we had made no contingency plan, some of the team members were confused and distressed as they had not been prepared for the possibility of staying behind. Others were greatly inconvenienced as they had made their way earlier to our destination only to find out upon arrival that the ministry had been cancelled. Where did we go wrong?'

Notice the opposition in this couple's mind between faith and reason. They saw them as incompatible, unhappy bedfellows. Operating on reason was seen as a 'lower standard'. See how planning was thought to be an evidence of unbelief. More specifically, planning that considered the possibility that the perceived will of God might not actually come to pass was seen as a sign of unbelief.

' "Come now, let us reason together," says the Lord' (Is 1:18). God calls us to use our reason. Too often we equate deeper spirituality with mindlessness. There lurks the suspicion—especially in the area of guidance—that to be spiritual means we never use our own judgement but are always led by direct words from the Lord. We suspect that reason is simply a second class substitute needed by those not spiritually 'sensitive' enough to be on the 'higher road' of hearing God's voice. If hearing God's voice has been consigned to the lunatic fringe then reason has too often been relegated to the austere ivory tower. Bring it in from the cold!

You may think rationality and sex to be an odd couple, but what they share in common is a place on the evangelical hit list. If the super-religious used to ban sex from church conversation, the super-spiritual now ban reason. Sex is being reinstated, so why not do the same for rationality? (On the subject of sex, J I Packer relates the story in his book, *Knowing God*, of how in 1949 the Pope asked Louis Armstrong whether he had any children. The Baptist jazzman replied, 'Not yet, but we're having a lot of fun trying.' The Pope greeted this with the good laugh it deserved.[8]) Give reason its proper place. We need not place it on the throne, but neither need we altogether banish it from the realm.

In responding to this couple I pointed out that it was not a question of either/or. One does not have to make a categorical decision between faith or reason. Both can be used. Reason is an ability and faith is an attitude. One can exercise an ability and hold an attitude simultaneously, whereas two attitudes often cannot be held at the same time. (Try being miserable and ecstatic at the same time. It cannot be done.) We can reason with faith or in unbelief. The mind is not the problem; our reasoning ability is not the problem. The underlying attitude is the problem. It is the unbelieving mind and faithless reason which are the real culprits. Where there is faith then reason becomes a tool to further the will of God. See the centurion in Matthew 8:5ff who asked to have his servant healed. His reasoning ability actually brought him closer to the heart of God because it was based on faith. He reasoned that if he himself had authority to speak and bring things to pass then how much more would this be true of the Son of God.

My other comment to this couple was that forming a contingency plan (ie, thinking in terms of the possible 'failure' of their primary plan) was not so much an exercise in unbelief as it was a function of wisdom. Notice that this is precisely what Moses did in Exodus 4:1: 'What if they do not believe me or listen to me. . . ?' The Lord responds not with a rebuke but with a miraculous staff! God has answers when we ask them. If one objects that Moses was not exactly the prime exemplar of a robust faith in God at this point in his life, what can one say to the Lord himself doing some contingency planning? He says, 'But if they do not believe these two signs . . . take some water . . . (it) will become blood. . .' (Ex 4:9). Fairly dramatic contingency planning! The Lord himself thought in terms of a back-up plan in case his first one did not work out.

A contingency plan is not only wise, it is also an expression of a humility which acknowledges that we may not have heard the Lord completely right. We may have missed important details or the timing. If that is possible, and who can doubt that it is not, we had better form a contingency plan.

## Counsellors counsel . . . not prophesy

Let's begin our look at what the Bible teaches about the relationship of our reasoning abilities to guidance by turning to one New Testament verse and one Old Testament verse. In Matthew 23:34 we read: 'Therefore I am sending you prophets and wise men and teachers.' In Ezekiel 7:26 it is written, 'They will try to get a vision from the prophet; the teaching of the law by the priest will be lost, as will the counsel of the elders.' Laid out in these two passages is a summary of the different ways in which God guides us:

1. *Prophet's vision*—Spirit the focus.
2. *Priest's teaching*—word the focus.
3. *Elders' counsel*—experience the focus.

Both Jesus and Ezekiel are listing three sources and types of godly direction and wisdom in the believer's life. First, there is the prophet's vision. The prophet was the one who spoke with a 'thus saith the Lord'. He was not giving his considered opinion; he was giving what God said. And rather than delivering the fruit of his meditations on the Scriptures he was proclaiming what the Spirit had told him. The Spirit was the source of his truth. God spoke directly to him rather than through the Scriptures or through his own thinking.

Second, there was the priest's teaching. Teachers were not prophets who heard the voice of the Spirit, but rather they were those who dug principles out of the word.

Methodical study rather than sudden inspiration was more their style. Their source of truth was primarily the Bible. While the Holy Spirit was still involved in this process, the involvement was of a more indirect fashion. The Holy Spirit could both strengthen their natural abilities of perception and give them flashes of insight in the midst of their meditations.

Thirdly, we have the elders' counsel. The most obvious mark of an elder was that he was 'elder'. And the chief benefit to be gained from being older was not rheumatism or grey hairs but experience. Having lived longer he had experienced more. The elder was not one of life's novices, full of sincere but untested idealism. There are some things that we can only really learn from experience. Theory we can learn without any experience; skills can only be learned by doing. Knowledge we can gain in an instant; deep-rooted wisdom takes time.

An elder's area of strength was not so much in hearing the Spirit or in being a Bible scholar but in the down-to-earth wisdom of years. He might not be able to foretell famines or reel off scriptures; his forte was the practical application of biblical truths to everyday experience.

Common sense characterises an elder. This is scriptural, as seen from Titus 1:8 (NASB) where one of the qualifications for an elder was that he was to be 'sensible'. (In the New International Version the Greek word is translated as 'self-controlled', and in the King James Version it is translated as 'sober'. Vine's expository dictionary says this word denotes a sound mind. The emphasis is good, solid thinking rather than airy-fairy spirituality.)

The elder was not so apt to utter the categorical 'thus saith the Lord' of the prophet, nor to declare the authoritative commands of Scripture (the teacher's role). His style was giving advice. He counselled. He gave insightful suggestions.

The differences between these three types of godly wisdom could be laid out like this:

| PROPHET USED: | TEACHER USED: | ELDER USED: |
|---|---|---|
| 100% revelation. | 33% revelation. | 33% revelation. |
| | 33% God-given ability to dig up biblical truth. | 33% God-given ability to discern biblical truths relation to life. |
| | 33% Bible focus. | 33% experience focus. |

This puts it crudely and hence not totally accurately—the prophet knew the Bible and learned from experience, and the teacher was not absolved from learning through life experiences—but it does communicate the right emphasis. If you went to a prophet to benefit from his ministry you would be looking for a word from the Lord and not a scholarly Bible study, whereas you would not expect a prophetic revelation from heaven when sitting under the ministry of a teacher. What you would expect from the teacher was teaching; an expanded understanding of the word of God.

While the prophet's ministry primarily operated in the realm of revelation, the teacher and wise man/elder operated out of a combination of an enlightened natural understanding infused with revelation insights as they looked at the Bible and at life. Rather than operating by minute-to-minute revelations the wise man had a God-given ability to discern within him. This is what God promised Solomon in 1 Kings 3:12: 'I will give you a wise and discerning heart. . . .'

But this discerning heart is not enough. We not only need the insights of our own hearts, no matter how wise, but the insights of God himself. And God has promised that to his people. In 2 Timothy 2:7 Paul states: 'Reflect on what I am saying, for the Lord will give you insight into all this.' Use your thinking on issues and as you do so the Lord will give flashes of insight.

## Second-Class Wisdom?

Both Ezekiel and Jesus point out that all three of these— prophecy, teaching and common sense—were sent by God. This means that they are all equally spiritual. If God sends it it can hardly be unspiritual. None are second-class or inferior. The man with the common sense can be just as spiritual as the man with the spectacular revelation.

Just look at the story of King David and Ahithophel in 2 Samuel 15–16. Outside of God, the key to this story is Ahithophel, not on his sword but on his counsel. Success or failure turns on how the rebel Absalom responds to Ahithophel's advice. His wisdom is essential. What sort of wisdom was it?

Ahithophel had the wisdom of a counsellor. He fits the category of 'wise men' Jesus spoke of in Matthew 23:34. Ahithophel's official position was that of 'king's counsellor' (2 Sam 15:12). This was a position completely distinct from 'king's prophet' (see 1 Chron 27.32–34 and 2 Chron 29:25). Their roles were quite different. The essence of the differences between them can be gleaned from the description of Ahithophel in 2 Samuel 16:23: 'Now in those days the advice Ahithophel gave was like that of one who enquires of God. That was how both David and Absalom regarded all of Ahithophel's advice.'

The wording is significant: 'like . . . one who enquires'. In other words, he did not enquire of the Lord! And yet the advice he gave was spot on and just as accurate as the word of a prophet. A prophet enquired of God, whereas a counsellor dipped into the deposit of wisdom God had placed within him. A counsellor exercised the gift of wisdom. He could insightfully weigh up situations.

So accurate were Ahithophel's assessments that even before a course of action was chosen he could see its outcome. And this was not because he had a 'word from God' or prophetic foresight but because he could deduce the logical conclusions of a given line of action. Thus, when his advice was rejected about pursuing David immediately he knew the final end would be defeat. Before one spear was thrown he knew that Absalom was a loser. The result? He committed suicide. Insight employed in the service of God's enemies is no blessing.

## Moses and Jethro

The story of Moses and his father-in-law Jethro in Exodus 18 also illustrates the key role that common sense advice plays in the kingdom of God. Moses, the busy leader who walked in intimate communion with God, was on the edge of burn-out. This is understandable when you consider that he had a counselling case-load of two-and-a-half-million people! God could have easily spoken to Moses about this situation in one of their face-to-face encounters, but he didn't. Notice how God brings a solution to him. God does not come on Sinai in a great cloud with a mightly revelation. No, he speaks through the common sense suggestions of a pagan priest. Jethro was a priest of Midian, the same Midian that led Israel astray in Numbers 31).

What advice did Jethro give that relieved Moses' burden? Was it some priceless jewel of revelation wisdom? No, it was a basic business principle called delegation. Jethro told Moses, 'But select capable men . . . appoint them as officials over thousands, hundreds, fifties, and tens. . . . That will make your load lighter, because they will share it with you' (Ex 18:21-22). Moses, the great man of revelation, needed Jethro and his common sense approach.

It would have been all too easy for Moses to have

responded to Jethro by saying, 'Who do you think you are? Don't you know you are speaking to God's man for the hour. I hear direct from God, and you dare advance this unspiritual piece of advice to me?' It was a measure of his humility that he didn't and was prepared to learn from anyone. It was another reason the Bible's verdict on him was that 'Moses was a very humble man, more humble than anyone else on the face of the earth' (Num 12:3). He did not reject the more natural sources of insight as inferior to spectacular revelations. He saw his need for all the gifts that God has given man, one of which is our rational mind, even when it sits in a pagan head. (We should note that though Jethro was the priest of an idolatrous nation, he was also a God-fearing man living up to the knowledge that he had. As soon as he saw who Jehovah was he honoured him as 'greater than all other gods' and brought him sacrifices [Ex 18:9–12]).

Jethro's common sense advice was so spot-on that it established a whole new institution in Israel: the judges. It was not only relevant for Moses but for following generations. This former slave nation was learning to rule itself, to judge itself. God used Jethro to introduce this new idea. We see God himself ratifying Jethro's advice a little later in Exodus 22:8 where he just assumes the existence of multiple judges besides Moses.

## Understanding is OK

Understanding is to be an attribute of God's people. The biblical ideal is not that we come to each situation with an empty mind. This is not what is meant by forsaking human wisdom and depending on God's wisdom. See what is said about Jesus in Luke 2:52: 'Jesus grew in wisdom. . . .' In other words he had an ever increasing stockpile of wisdom, of godly principles that he kept adding to as he grew up. When he was faced with a situation he did not come at it with an empty mind and then simply hear the voice of the Spirit giving him the relevant bit of information. No, he listened to the Spirit *and* he drew from the stockpile of wisdom he had been building up since his youth.

Jesus was no fool. See him in Luke 2:47 at the green age of twelve amazing the scribes with his understanding. And remember that Jesus never lost an argument. (I could do with that ability when it comes to my wife!) In Matthew 22 the Pharisees try twice to catch Jesus out, first on the question of paying taxes, and second on marriage in the future. Having slipped out of their intellectual mousetrap Jesus then goes on the offensive himself and gives them a scriptural brain-teaser. It's riposte and lunge . . . or as a friend of mine puts it: 'Scriptures at ten paces'. While it is true that Jesus was being guided by the Holy Spirit in these instances, we also see here the evidence of a quick and active mind that has learned to think God's thoughts.

The Bible does not tell us that we should not make judgements or use our rational minds in the guidance process. Proverbs 3:5 tells us: 'lean not on your own understanding'. This is not the same thing as not using our own understanding. Leaning speaks of where we are putting our ultimate trust, and what we are resting our entire weight upon to support us. Our limited reason unaided by God will never be a sufficient source of guidance for a person's life. At best, human wisdom is good but limited. At worst, it is misleading and destructive. So don't lean on it but rather lean on a God who finds it downright difficult to be wrong.

To equate 'not leaning' with 'not using' our mind is a misinterpretation of Scripture. It would be like interpreting Matthew 6's injunction not to be concerned about tomorrow as saying that we must not think about tomorrow. This is to confuse underlying attitudes with overt actions. In Matthew 6, Jesus is not forbidding bank savings or attendance at summer sales as being evidences of 'worrying about tomorrow'. He is getting at the attitude of worry, the underlying motivation for our actions.

So in Proverbs 3:5 the writer is not making a point about the inherent ungodliness of human thought; he is not focusing on the action of thinking, but rather on the underlying attitude of trust. That's really what his concern is, and that's really what God's concern is. As Bob Mumford has said, God wants independent thinkers with dependent spirits.

Far from instructing us to abandon our understanding, the Bible actually tells us to develop it! Too often we polarise the rational from the miraculous. The Bible seems to think they can fit together quite cosily. How ironical that the command to develop our minds is found in that portion of Scripture devoted to the more 'mystical' gifts. It is in 1 Corinthians 14:20 that the command comes to us, 'Brothers, stop thinking like children. In regard to evil be infants, but in your thinking be adults.' Please note the phrase: 'in your thinking be adults.' The thing that marks an adult off from a child is the word 'development'. An adult is simply a child who has grown up. No new faculties are there. He has not been given an extra head along the way or anything like that. He has simply developed physically, emotionally, and mentally what has always been there. So Paul is telling the Corinthians to grow up in their thinking, to develop it.

Paul wanted these Corinthian Christians to have active, sharp minds. In his epistles Paul not only gives advice flowing from heavenly revelations but counsel that is down-to-earth common sense. His advice on how to take up a collection in 1 Corinthians 16:2 is the height of practicality. So too is his counsel on circumcision in 1 Corinthians 7:18: 'Was a man already circumcised when he was called? He should not become uncircumcised.' That sounds fairly common-sensical. He could hardly do otherwise!

## Understanding liberates

We need to be clear that we are free to use our minds for two important reasons. Firstly, it will free us from worry. If we think that we are meant to get everything from the Spirit in revelation, we will be continually walking under a cloud of worry and condemnation. There are just too many things God wants us to decide about ourselves, things which he will not show us by his Spirit. I can well recall as a young Christian daily waiting on God, asking him what section of the Bible I should be reading that day. Frustration would mount as I seemed to be only greeted with silence. In desperation, I resorted to picking out sections of my own choosing. (Who wants to spend twenty minutes finding out what to read and only ten minutes actually reading it?) But really I felt this was a defeat, and in the back of my mind I would be nagged with the doubt that I might well be missing God's will. I mean, what if I was reading in the wrong place? Maybe God wanted to speak to me out of Matthew and here was I toiling through Exodus. Maybe I would be missing out on hearing God. Panic! I can see now that my difficulty was simply a misunderstanding of the place of personal judgement in guidance. God wanted me to just make up my own mind where I read.

This is the way we live. We do use our minds. It is impossible to escape doing so. An 'over-spiritual' view is hard to live with. The tension between the ideal and the real is too great. It's rather like the western intellectuals of the 1930s who idolised 'Uncle Joe' Stalin's workers' paradise in Russia. One of these intellectuals, Lincoln Steffens, said, '. . . I am a patriot for Russia; the future is there; Russia will win out and it will save the world. That is my belief. But I don't want to live there.' High flying ideals, but he had to come to terms with the reality.

If we find that we are not living our beliefs there are two possibilities: either our living is not good enough or our theory is not good enough. A theology that does not give place to the mind in guidance is a theory that is not good enough. Being unable to live with it (ie, trying to avoid all decision making in favour of revelation) we are then forced into hypocrisy in an effort to seem spiritual, or into condemnation as we fail to live up to our standards. Thi hardly seems to be the fruit of the Spirit.

The second reason we are defending reason's place is that using our minds will actually help us find God's will. Here is a thought for us: common sense is a gift from God and not a trick of the devil. It is something God has given us to cope with life and should not be seen as a decoy the devil has planted to throw us off the track.

A scriptural view of guidance should combine both the divine and the human dimensions. It includes both the divine and definite 'thus saith the Lord', and the human and tentative 'my opinion is'. It is important to see that it is not wrong to make decisions based on our own limited, human opinions. This element of the human and tentative figured largely in the apostle Paul's decision making processes.

## Paul's planning process

Romans 1:13: '. . . I planned many times to come to you (but have been prevented from doing so until now) in order that I might have a harvest among you.' We can make three observations from this verse:

1. Making rational plans for the future was not seen as unspiritual by Paul.

2. We see the combination of the human and the divine in Paul's style of seeking guidance. In forming his future itinerary Paul was as involved as God was. It was Paul who planned the trip and not just God.

3. Paul saw the area of guidance as not only including divine and definite revelations, but also as encompassing tentative decisions made according to the best of our

ability. It is for this reason that Paul is not deeply upset when his plans do not work out. We do not find him castigating himself saying, 'Oh I've gone out of the will of God and gone ahead of him. I must have been planning in the flesh.' Instead, he has a refreshingly matter-of-fact approach whereby he just accepts this hitch in his plans. He knows his own fallible thinking was involved in these plans, but he is at his ease knowing that God gives room for this. And then he goes right back to making some more plans.

Romans 15:23–24: 'But now that there is no more place for me to work in these regions, and since I have been longing for many years to see you, I plan to do so when I go to Spain. I hope to visit you while passing through and to have you assist me on my journey there, after I have enjoyed your company for a while.' This verse is instructive on several counts.

1. We see once again the legitimate place of the human element as well as the divine. See how much of Paul is involved in this: 'I have been longing . . . I plan . . . I hope. . .' The language here is not about what God is saying but about what Paul wants. Paul does not find it necessary to put all his own desires in neutral and be an 'empty channel' for God.

2. We see again the legitimate place Paul gives to the rational mind as well as to revelation. Paul does not give as the reason for his decision that 'God has told me'. Rather he says, 'there is no more place for me to work . . . and since I have been longing . . . to see you'. In other words, he has decided on rational grounds that he should come. In this case those rational grounds were that he had no more opportunity to work he knew God did not want his gifts to lie dormant and unused, so he looked for an open door where he could bless others and use those gifts. His personal desires were also thrown into the mix: 'since I have been longing . . . to see you'. Again we see that guidance is not just a matter of divine revelation.

1 Corinthians 16:2–8 displays the same elements noted above.

1. The language of reason predominates over the language of revelation. He is staying on at Ephesus 'because a great door for effective work has opened'. This is a scriptural way of putting the common sense adage: 'Strike while the iron is hot.' Paul goes on to say that he will bring some men along, not on the basis of revelation but 'if it seems advisable'.

2. The human element looms large. See how often the word 'I' is used. It is not only God who is making the plans but also Paul taking the initiative according to his judgement and desires. The Lord can check him if he wants—'I hope to spend some time with you, if the Lord permits'—but Paul is not passively waiting for God to show his will. He is actively making plans. He holds them lightly—'Perhaps I will stay with you'—but he still has them.

Acts 15 also provides us with an insight on how the early church went about finding God's will on issues. A controversy arose over the question of circumcision. Some of the early believers felt strongly that they should be circumcised, while others, including Paul, held equally strongly to the opposite position. How was God's will to be found on the matter? Interestingly, they did not spend most of their time in a prayer meeting waiting upon God for a supernatural revelation (though I am sure they prayed). Rather, their approach was to think about it and discuss it—the much maligned 'committee meeting'! 'The apostles and elders met to consider this question. After much discussion. . .' (Acts 15:6–7). They talked about it, and they examined the question from different angles, each one giving his own opinion. That may not sound so spiritual, but nevertheless that is exactly what the pillars of our faith did.

After listening to the different arguments how did they finally decide on the right course of action? They made a personal judgement: 'It is my judgement, therefore. . .' (v 19). They used their minds and did not seem to think they were presuming on the will of God. Indeed, so confident were they that they had arrived at the will of God through using their personal judgement that they said, 'It seemed good to the Holy Spirit and to us. . .' (v 28). Rather than opposing the mystical and the rational, the supernatural and the natural, the early church seemed comfortable with both, and that was due to their conviction that God was comfortable with both.

## Balance

Balance is what we want. Now if you are like me you could almost scream at the mention of the word 'balance'. It can be such a sneaky word. When one Christian disagrees with another Christian's emphasis, how much better to call him 'unbalanced' rather than 'heretical' (too shrill) or 'wrong' (too crudely blunt). You effectively torpedo the other's view while playing it safe yourself. I mean, who wants to believe something that is 'unbalanced'? It sounds suspiciously close to being insane. The label 'unbalanced' is our modern-day equivalent to the earlier tag of 'leper' . . . untouchable! It is such a safe way to disagree because while throwing suspicion on another's view you are still able to maintain your own reputation for being eminently reasonable, fair-minded, and charitably struggling to go along with the other fellow's viewpoint as far as one can. What a nice fellow! The veneer of civility is firmly in place. 'No hysterical, crazed "heresy-under-every-bush type" am I.'

Plus, how slippery and hard to grapple with is this word 'unbalanced'. It has no hard corners but is all haze and shadow. When you label a viewpoint as unbalanced it usually means that you don't actually disagree with its content but rather with the emphasis given to that viewpoint. Content one can deal with, but how do you argue with an emphasis? Emphasis focuses not on what you say but on how you say it. 'Wrong' is crisp, clear and objective; either yes or no. 'Balance' is hazy, vague and subjective, dealing with the middle ground between yes and no.

'Balance' can be just another unexamined buzz word that we throw around in the same manner as we do words like 'middle class'. The person has somehow been contaminated by the accusation, though nobody knows exactly what the accusation is.

One man's balance is another man's compromise. Translated, balance may mean nothing more than that which I believe in, and unbalanced means nothing more than what I don't believe in. Balance becomes not what is biblical but simply what I am used to; what I am comfortable living with. Let's face it, nobody thinks they are unbalanced, not even the raving heretic. He just thinks everybody else is unbalanced.

Balance is not always desirable. Should we balance righteousness with a little unrighteousness? Was Abraham unbalanced when he left all to travel God-knows-where (literally)?

Yes, there is a need for biblical balance that takes heed of the 'whole counsel of God'. I am not advocating that we all strike the word balance from our dictionaries or purge our language of this distasteful word. I am much too balanced for that! It is difficult to live with two extremes. How much simpler to toss out one side rather than continue with this juggling act, keeping two truths going simultaneously. Juggling is not something that comes naturally to us, but nevertheless it is something we all have to do. So let's hold these 'truths in tension', whether in the area of God's sovereignty and man's responsibility, God's severity and God's kindness, or guidance through our thinking and guidance that supercedes our rational processes.

Balance is important if we are to walk in God's ways in guidance. Have you ever tried to walk with only one

leg? Possible but awkward. So guidance will come more
smoothly when we use both the proffered legs. God wants
to speak to us outside of our own independent thinking
and he wants to use the brains he has given us. As
someone has said, if you give your son a watch you don't
expect him to keep asking you the time.

The trick is to have a theology that opens us to the
possibility of both thinking and revelation while developing a discernment as to which mode of operating is
more appropriate at any given time. If our theology tells
us that reason is second class or that revelation is passé
then we will not expect God to guide us through these
means. And, 'According to your faith will it be done to
you' (Mt 9:29) means that God will not speak to us in
that way, not because he does not want to but because
we won't believe that he can or will.

God does not lead us all in the same way. Some he
may lead in fine details (type and colour co-ordination of
clothing, for instance), and for others he may not. Do not
feel superior (the 'I've-arrived-spiritually-though-I-would-
never-put-it-so-bluntly' syndrome), or inferior if you are
not led in the same way. Be challenged and be taught by
the way God leads others, but do not necessarily copy.
Realise that God has a personal path in guidance for you.
We want to learn from each other but ultimately look to
God for his way for us. Remember again Jesus' directive
to Peter who was enquiring about the Lord's path for the
apostle John: 'If I want him to . . . what is that to you?
You must follow me' (Jn 21:22).

As our opinions concerning 'true spirituality' can either
hinder or help us feel free to operate in both revelation
and reason, this will be the next subject we look at.

# 6

## *True Spirituality*

Anybody here wanting to be unspiritual please raise your hand. One does not need to be a far-sighted prophet to predict that few will respond—at least not among the readers of a book like this. No one wants to be unspiritual or (even worse!) to be thought unspiritual. We would hate to find ourselves on the receiving end of the charge Paul flung at the Corinthian Christians; 'Brothers, I could not address you as spiritual but as worldly—mere infants in Christ. I gave you milk, not solid food, for you were not yet ready for it' (1 Cor 3:1–2). Ouch! The sting lies in the accusation of mediocrity. Their problem was not that they were not Christians, but that they were stunted, undeveloped, second-rate Christians; 'mere infants' Paul calls them. We have those who are flying first class—the spiritual ones—and we have those who are going second class—the unspiritual ones. Those hungry for all that God has got laid on will quite naturally recoil from mediocre, mush Christianity. And in this we reflect the heart of God who once told his people, 'So, because you are lukewarm—neither hot nor cold—I am about to spit you out of my mouth' (Rev 3:16). One gets the idea that doing something halfway is not one of God's more favoured subjects. Do it and do it well.

Yes, reaching for spirituality and avoiding unspirituality

is healthy and normal for the Christian. Our problem lies
not in agreeing on this goal but in defining this goal. We
know the goal is right; we are not so clear on what it is!
Now this presents a problem. Imagine a marksman trying
to aim for a target that he knows exists, but doesn't know
quite where it is. It is very difficult to hit the mark, and
frustrating if you are conscientious. So what are we aiming
at when we aim at spirituality? What is our picture of
spirituality? What do we imagine a spiritual person looks
like? Is he always serious and sober (the picture in bygone
days), or is he perpetually smiling and happy (our modern
picture)? Is he a mystic who, head in the clouds, disdains
the hurly-burly of everyday life? Or is he an activist,
overloaded with church activities, who never 'wastes his
time' in frivolous recreations? In regards to guidance, is
the spiritual Christian the one who hears voices or gets
exact details down to what shoes he should wear or at
which restaurant table he should seat himself? Just what
is spirituality?

Basically, the Bible teaches what we could call 'whole
man spirituality'. Spirituality is not about leaving our
humanness behind and becoming some sort of other-
worldly spectre. It is about letting God invade and have
his way in all parts of our human personality. It is about
becoming more human. It is positive, not negative.

## The nature of man

To spell out just what this means we need to examine the
biblical picture of man. It is out of our concept of man,
how he functions, and how God has designed him to
function that we build our concept of spirituality. If our
concept of the nature of man is cloudy then our concept
of spirituality will be cloudy. If our notions on the proper
functioning of man's inner nature are wrong then our
notions on spirituality will be wrong.

The Bible teaches that man has a three-part nature: the

body, the soul and the spirit. Paul writes in 1 Thessalonians 5:23: 'May God . . . sanctify you. . . . May your whole spirit, soul and body be kept blameless. . .' He mentions three distinct natures. Hebrews 4:12 says: 'For the word of God . . . penetrates even to dividing soul and spirit. . . .' This verse states that the soul and spirit are divisible. Rather than soul and spirit being two different ways of describing the same thing, they seem more to be two quite distinct entities. The difference between them is so subtle that only the word of God can divide them. Their difference is almost imperceptible, but it does exist. With our imperfect perceptions, you and I may not be able to say, 'This is where the soul ends and the spirit begins,' but the word of God can. We may not even be able to describe exactly what the difference is between the soul and the spirit, but what the Scripture settles for us is that they are different.

It is one thing to state that man has three distinct natures. It is another matter altogether to assign functions to each of these natures. Here the Scriptures speak less clearly. Nevertheless they must have their respective functions. The functions of the physical nature as distinct from the soul nature are easy enough. We would not hesitate to assign eating and digesting as a function of the body. We would feel secure in saying it is not mainly a function of the mind or the emotions. We are not so confident in the realms of the spirit and the soul. When I am thinking is my soul operating or is my spirit operating? This is not merely an academic question but one with practical implications, as we will see when we proceed.

Let's look at one suggested model of the nature of man purporting to show the function of man's three part-nature and how these functions were meant to interrelate:

The functions of the human spirit are said to be intuition, conscience and communion. Intuition is knowing something directly and not as the result of rational, deductive mental processes. We just 'know' for

| SPIRIT | | |
|--------|--------|--------|
| Intuition | Conscience | Communion |

| SOUL | | |
|-----------|--------|---------|
| Intellect | Will | Emotion |

| BODY | | |
|-------|------|-------|
| Flesh | Bone | Blood |

instance that we love somebody, but we would be at a loss if we were asked to prove that we loved them. Our conviction of the existence of right and wrong is not something that we work out logically, but is rather an intuitive certainty built into us by God.

Conscience is the ability to discern right from wrong. It acts as our internal judge and jury. Seen as a nuisance by some it is actually one of the jewels in man's crown. It is an attribute that sets him off as unique from the brutes of the forest.

Worship or communion is the ability to touch God directly through our spirits. Communion is more than a transmission of information; it is an actual 'meeting' with God. It is what enables us to sense the presence of God.

The functions of the soul of man are claimed to be mind, will and emotion. The mind is the main communication centre of our personality. It acts as a kind of clearing house for all ideas that come our way, sorting out the wheat from the chaff. This is where our critical abilities reside.

The will is what gives force and drive to us. It is the motor of our personalities. With it we decide what we will not do and what we will do. It translates ideas into reality.

Emotion is what adds richness to life. Mind gives content, but emotion gives atmosphere. It makes us sensitive to a whole side of life that the more critical faculties of the mind can be completely oblivious to.

The functions of the body are clear to most of us so I need not detail them.

## The Spirit rules, OK?

If these are the functions of man's three natures then what is their interrelationship meant to look like? We shall first address in this chapter the widely held view that these three natures were designed to function in a kind of hierarchy, with the spirit ruling the soul which then rules the body. Let me spell out more fully this view.

It is thought that before the Fall God by his Holy Spirit communicated to man's spirit which then communicated to man's soul which then communicated to man's body. Man lived not only in harmony with nature but also with himself because he was functioning according to his original design. The spirit held pride of place.

When man fell in the garden of Eden he not only fell out of harmony with God, but also with himself. No longer did his spirit rule his soul and his soul his body. Now man's bodily appetites ruled his soul, his soul growing enslaved in the process. As to man's spirit, well, that was dead so it could hardly rule his soul any more. Disintegration occurred as sin intervened and the human spirit was cut off from God. Man's whole being was built around his spirit. It was through his spirit that he had contact with God. But sin threw all of this out of kilter.

Anarchy resulted. Every part of man's nature now strove for rule.

From the Fall onwards man's spirit took the back seat. No longer did man perceive first by his spirit, to be followed by his soul, and his body reacting last of all. Now man ceased living out of his spirit. This is why writers like Watchman Nee have described our pre-Christian fallen state as 'soulish' that is, unconverted man was not only living an immoral life, but also a distorted life. He no longer lived out of his spirit but out of his soul. The key part of his personality, the spirit, was not being allowed to express its ruling function. The obvious conclusion is that not only is it vital to learn a new moral lifestyle forsaking sin, but it is equally vital to learn a new 'spiritual' lifestyle in which we forsake soulish ways of leading our lives, and in which our spirits rule us once again.

While the above model has some aspects to recommend it I hesitate to fully endorse it. My reservations are as follows:

1. The exact functions of the human spirit and soul are not so neatly and sharply laid out in the Scriptures as they are in the above scheme.

2. Scripture nowhere spells out that the spirit rules the soul, and the soul rules the body. Not only is Scripture silent on such a scheme, but this view actually contradicts Scripture at several points.

Far from Scripture neatly laying out and dividing up the functions of soul and spirit, the Scriptures show the spirit exercising faculties are said to be functions of the soul. We will also see the soul performing activities that are said to belong to the spirit. The whole man seems to be exercised in these human reactions rather than mainly the soul or the spirit. Look at the following verses:

Matthew 26:41: 'The spirit is willing. . .' But it has been claimed that will is a function of the soul.

Luke 1:47: 'My soul praises (communion) . . . my spirit

rejoices (emotion). . . .' Again the assigned functions are reversed.

John 11:33: '. . . he was deeply moved in spirit. . . .' The spirit is capable of emotion. Emotion is evidently not simply a function of the soul.

Genesis 41:8: '(Pharaoh's) spirit was troubled. . . .' This is the New American Standard Bible's more literal translation of the New International Version's 'his mind was troubled'. The Hebrew word is 'ruach', the same word that is used in 'Holy Spirit'. Again we see an emotion arising out of our spirit and not just out of our soul. It is also interesting to note that an unregenerated man's spirit was active. To be spiritually dead does not then mean that our spirits are not functioning. It seems to mean just that we are judicially dead, under the sentence of death, condemned men, and separated from God, which is a living death.

Proverbs 14:29: '. . . he that is hasty of spirit exalteth folly.' This is the King James Version's more literal rendering of what the New International Version translates as a 'quick-tempered man'. Again the Hebrew word used is 'ruach'. The point relevant to us here is that once again an emotion—anger—is seen as a function of the spirit and not primarily of the soul.

Of course it is not crucially important in itself to correctly pigeon-hole all the activities of the human personality; to argue endlessly over whether emotion is a function of the spirit or the soul. We would then be repeating the mistake of those medieval theologians who clashed heads by the hour over how many angels could fit on the head of a pin. We are not interested in dry, academic arguments for arguments' sake. We *are* interested in understanding what spirituality is.

My second reservation concerns the supposed ruling role of the human spirit over the rest of man, that man sorted out, or 'spiritual man', lives with his spirit ruling his soul. The obverse is also thought to be true, that soulish man allows his soul to dictate to his spirit. The practical outworking of this belief is too often an unhealthy suspicion of the mind. Its effect on guidance is to elevate as spiritual those insights which come to us via intuition (such as words of knowledge and prophecy) and to denigrate those insights which come to us via the mind. A 'hunch' that comes in a flash tends to be seen as a few steps closer to heaven than a conclusion that has been painstakingly worked out by rational processes. As an old poet said, such hunches are seen as descending upon us 'trailing clouds of glory'. Rational deductions, by contrast, seem utterly pedestrian and boringly earthly. Exemplifying this sort of thinking are the following quotes from a book on guidance:

Nowhere does the Bible say he (God) will guide us through our mentality. The Bible does not say that the mind of man is the candle of the Lord. It says that the spirit of man is the candle of the Lord.[9]

The Holy Spirit abiding in our spirits must communicate with us through our spirits—not through our minds. That is why your spirit knows things your head doesn't. . . . The reason . . . believers continually miss it and make mistakes . . . is because our spirits which should guide us are kept locked away in prison. Knowledge, or intellect, has taken the throne.'[10]

The priority given to the spirit and its functions is clear. Spirit (small 's') is seen as superior to soul. This same priority is nowhere more clear than in the writings of that man of God Watchman Nee. When it comes to his life I cannot hold a candle to the man. But when it comes to his theology I must hold the light of God's word up to it. I am not a believer in the crusades and certainly do not wish to embark on one against Watchman Nee. It is simply that he puts this theology in such conveniently stark, either/or terms that he, more than most, forces us to define exactly what we do or do not believe in this area.

Here are some of the statements found in his three volume work, *The Spiritual Man*:

> It is not sin alone but all which belongs to the soulish which is defiled and defiling . . . resist it. . . . As soon as the soul stirs the spirit suffers and will resist right away.[11]

> To live by the spirit means to walk according to intuition (versus noble feelings or the loftiest thoughts). . . . The Holy Spirit does not operate directly on our minds.[12]

> Nothing is of any spiritual benefit unless it flows from revelation . . . from the spirit. . . . If we walk according to sudden thoughts, to our natural inclinations then we are activating the old man again.[13]

> It is important to understand that the Holy Spirit dwells in man's depths (deeper than thoughts, feelings, decisions) or else man shall seek God's guidance in his soul.[14]

So that which is of the soul is bad; it is 'soulish', an important word in Watchman Nee's vocabulary.[15] It must be said that the Bible never speaks in terms of man living 'out of his spirit' or in terms of 'his spirit ruling his soul'. It does speak of the spiritual man in contrast to the natural man, but it does not define spiritual man in the terms we see above. Spiritual man is he who is ruled by the Holy Spirit, not he who is ruled by his own spirit.

Yes, there will be times when—if we provisionally accept the capabilities which have been suggested we assign to the spirit and soul—my spirit will rule over my soul in the form of my intuition telling my rebellious mind what to do (or where to get off!). But equally there are times when soul will rule and, quite properly, override my spirit.

Consider the following examples:

1. Sometimes my conscience (spirit) is wrong and will need to be overruled by my mind (soul). My conscience

may be completely darkened or just misinformed—what the Bible calls a 'weak' conscience (1 Cor 8:7). In either case the mind needs to take charge and re-educate the conscience.

2. Sometimes my will (soul) needs to take charge over my communing ability (spirit). I may want to stay and read my Bible, have fellowship and go to prayer meetings, all the while neglecting some ordinary household chores that I need to discipline myself to do.

3. At another time my intuition (spirit) may give me some wonderful assessment of an idea, a person, or a situation which my mind (soul) tells me is wrong and unbiblical. So my mind overrules my intuition. In 1 Corinthians 14:15–19, 26–33, Paul is basically subjecting their mystical experience to a rational critique. He is correcting their intuitions and desire for communion according to the dictates of the mind. And in Galatians 1:8 Paul warns the Galatians that no matter how spiritual the source (angels in this case) the main consideration is the content, the message. It's not mind over matter, but mind over spirit!

4. Moving even further down the scale we see that even my body can legitimately rule my soul and spirit. My oversensitive conscience and unrealistic mind may tell me I can and should shoulder more responsibilities than God wants me to cope with. My body may break down under the strain. Christians do suffer from exhaustion, burn-out, and even nervous breakdowns. God could well be speaking to us through our bodies. They are giving us a message if we would only listen. St Francis of Assisi used to call his body 'Brother Ass'. Remember how God could use even use an ass to communicate to his servant Balaam? Rather than beat it relentlessly, listen to your own Balaam's ass.

The proper, scriptural order is not necessarily one where the Holy Spirit communicates first to our spirits which then communicate to our minds (soul). Perhaps the

Holy Spirit will speak a thought first to our mind and only secondly do we take it up into our intuition or spirit. Surely this is what happens in a slow, struggling worship time when God speaks in prophecy and, as a result of the word which we take in initially through our minds, the worship then 'takes off'. We commune with God (a spirit function) because of a communication that came to us through our minds (a soul function).

Contrary to Watchman Nee's suggestion, the Holy Spirit does operate directly on our minds. Indeed, what is the 'still, small voice' (see Chapter 4) but God speaking directly into our minds. However, Watchman Nee is correct when he says that the Holy Spirit operates directly on our spirits; this is what a 'witness of the Spirit' is. Neither mode of communication is better or more 'spiritual'. If God does it, it is spiritual. The important point is not 'how' he communicated but 'that' he communicated.

## Mishmash theory

Rather than a clear hierarchy in which the spirit rules over the rest of man, we have presented to us a much more mixed-up portrait. I call it the 'mishmash theory' of human personality. It may not be neat and tidy, yet it possesses one distinct advantage: it better represents what actually happens with man.

The biblical picture is not that man's spirit needs to be restored to its rightful place of rule, but that God's Spirit needs to be restored to his rightful place of rule. A person steeped in the occult may be living very much out of their spirit—having plenty of demonic intuitions and experiencing a lot of communion, only with the wrong spirits—and yet they are still not living according to the biblical pattern. The Bible's concern is not that we should walk according to our spirit but that we should walk 'according to the Spirit' (Rom 8:4). The focus is not on us but on God; not on what particular part of our personality we are using, but on whether we are submitting our whole personality—body, soul and spirit—to God. *He* rules; *not* our spirits! That is the real point. The need is not primarily for us to listen to our spirits, but for us to listen to God's Spirit in whatever way he chooses to communicate—whether through our body or soul or spirit. This is what spirituality is about.

The absurdity of focusing on 'spirituality-as-listening-to-our-spirit' as opposed to 'spirituality-as-listening-to-God' can be seen if we think of a Christian being tempted by the devil through his intuition. Let's say that he 'intuits' that he ought to divorce his wife, leave his kids and marry that pretty young filly he met at the local dance. His mind tells him that the word of God states that divorce and adultery is wrong. If we focus on 'spirituality-as-listening-to-your-spirit' we would be forced to say that it was more 'spiritual' for him to leave his wife. Any warning bells going? I hope so.

As suggested at the beginning of this chapter, when man fell his spirit fell too. But its fall was not a sort of coup d'etat where man's spirit was toppled from the throne of his personality. The Fall did not result in man's spirit being demoted down the organisational chart within man. Top-dog-spirit did not become bottom-dog-spirit only to find its place taken by that ambitious soul of his. The problem that has been ours since the Fall is not that the spirit's contributions are no longer regarded as authoritative but that the spirit's contributions are now sullied by sin.

And this is no more than what has happened to the whole of man. It is not just man's spirit which fell but man's spirit/soul/body; the whole house came crashing down. The mind was darkened, the will enslaved and weakened, and the emotions perverted. The body also suffered. It became a victim of disease and, even worse, mortality. The fall was not about whether man was listening to his soul but about whether he was listening to

Satan. And Satan has no vendetta against our spirits. He'll use anything—spirit, soul, body—to get at us. His vendetta is against man as a whole. If anything, he envies us for our bodies more than for our spirits. It is the one thing he does not have. He needs bodies to 'possess' to give him a vehicle for expression on earth.

Rather than seeing man as consisting of a hierarchy of capabilities with the spirit ruling on top—an internal monarchy—I would suggest that man is a type of internal democracy with all the facets of his personality having equal weight and say. Sometimes one aspect is listened to and sometimes another according to the validity of their contribution. To use another picture, it is not that the spirit is the bishop and the soul is the obedient board of deacons. Rather, we should conceive of the spirit and soul as a board of elders co-equal in authority, the presiding elder not being our spirit but the Lord. The human spirit and soul are on the same level before God. The key is submission—not of the soul to the spirit but of the spirit and soul to God.

## Terminological confusion strikes again

Compounding our misunderstanding of spirituality is the fact that the word 'spiritual' carries two different meanings. In this it is similar to the biblical word 'flesh' which sometimes refers to our physical bodies and sometimes to our sinful tendencies. Because some have not kept this double meaning of the word 'flesh' clearly in mind, the Bible has been misinterpreted as condemning the physical body. The word 'spiritual' has met a similiar fate. Misunderstanding dogs it because it can mean two very different things. It can mean:

1. *Substance*—what part (or substance) of our human personality are we using in a given activity.

But this word can also relate to:

2. *Values*—what we are doing as right or wrong, good or bad.

To avoid misunderstanding we need to ask which of these two senses we are using when we use the word 'spiritual'.

Let me use an example to clarify what I mean. A new word was drafted into the English language in the 1960s; this was the word 'heavy'. Prior to this time 'heavy' always described a physical reality; it described substance. More specifically, it described weight. Before the 1960s, if upon being told, 'Watch out, I've got something heavy for you,' you had rolled up your sleeve, hitched up your belt and prepared yourself for some heavy exertion, this would have been deemed a perfectly appropriate response. In the 60s you would have been thought mad or just hopelessly out of touch. 'I've got a heavy record,' now meant something completely different. What happened? A word that once only related to substance now took on meanings relating to value and aesthetic effect. The same word can have completely different connotations.

Now, this ability of language to have double meanings is an altogether innocent property. Its innocence is only lost when it effects us adversely in practical areas. Say a friend had told you he had a bunch of 'really heavy' records he wanted you to listen to and you, as a consequence, hired a van to pick them up . . . only to find three records on your arrival. You would then be out of pocket of some hard earned cash. All of a sudden exact word definitions would take on more than academic meaning to you.

The word 'spiritual' lends itself to this sort of confusion. For instance, one Bible teacher has written, 'An intuition is fallible but it is spiritual.'[16] Let us analyse this. We can use the word spiritual as meaning 'that activity which comes from the part or substance of man called the spirit'. It is spiritual because it is our spirits which are being exercised. In this sense, intuition is spiritual.

But a second meaning for spiritual is 'that which is of God, which is in line with his ways and which is therefore pleasing to him' (a value judgement). Used in this way a spiritual activity is simply one that God approves of, irrespective of whether the activity engages our spirits or our bodies. Here, intuition might well be unspiritual. For instance, if intuition tells us to do something contrary to the will of God it would be unspiritual. It would be urging us to do something out of tune with God, and you cannot get much more unspiritual than that. Intuition can thus be both spiritual (as relating to substance) and spiritual (as relating to values) at the same time. Clear as mud?

The problem enters when we use the word in sense one, but it gets taken as meaning sense two, or vice versa. Terminological confusion sets in![17] An act like feeding the hungry and clothing the naked is spiritual in sense two (God values it) but unspiritual in sense one (the substance involved is physical, not spiritual). If we are asked whether feeding the poor was a spiritual activity, strictly speaking we should not answer 'yes' or 'no' but, 'In what way do you mean spiritual?' Is gardening spiritual or unspiritual? Again, we can answer with a resounding, 'It depends'. It depends on how the word 'spiritual' is being used. It is unspiritual in the sense that it is dealing with a non-spirit-substance called dirt ('soil' to any self-respecting gardener), but it is spiritual in terms of values, ie, in reflecting God's ways and priorities. That gardening is not unspiritual (in value terms) is only too obvious from the stress God originally placed on it in the Garden of Eden. (What else do you do in a garden?) It was to be Adam's main activity. God liked it! And there cannot be anyone more spiritual than God. Beware of any conclusions that make you out to be more spiritual than God.

In relating all this to guidance, we must beware the superficially plausible conclusion that guidance received via the mind is soulish and unspiritual, while guidance received via the spirit is spiritual. That is unbiblical, confused thinking, arising from a failure to make a distinction between the two meanings of 'spiritual'.

Sometimes it is the height of spirituality to exercise our souls. Take 1 Corinthians 14:12–17 as an example. In this passage the Apostle Paul is instructing the church on the best and most God-pleasing way (and therefore the most spiritual way) to conduct public worship. The question is how much they should pray with their spirits, in tongues, and how much to pray with their minds. Paul points out that it is unhelpful to pray only with their spirit as, 'You may be giving thanks well enough, but the other man is not edified' (v 17). He essentially says to them to get out of their spirits and into their minds. This is what is spiritual in this situation. How ironical; it is unspiritual to be too spiritual!

Paul does contrast the natural or soulish man with the spiritual man in 1 Corinthians 2:14–15. The key difference between them is not in who exercises their soul but in who listens to God. Receiving input from the Holy Spirit is what constitutes spirituality. The solution to soulishness is not found in killing our souls but in coming alive to the Holy Spirit as he works through our spirits or our souls.

I have been focusing on the possible overemphasis on the spirit, on intuition over reason, because our concentration in this chapter has been on counteracting a false view of spirituality. Of course, all I have said can equally be applied the other way around. That is, just as some devalue the place of reason others devalue the proper place of intuition. And others exalt reason over emotion (a legacy of our scientific worldview against which the western world has been in revolt for the last thirty years). What we want is to allow each aspect of our personality to be released to give their valid contributions. 'There is a time for everything, and a season for every activity under heaven,' the good book says (Eccles 3:1).

If we want to avoid condemnation and confusion when

we hear terms like spiritual and soulish, then we will be well advised to ask in what sense the word is being used, whether it is in the purely descriptive sense or in the value-laden sense. The penalty for not doing so is devaluing activities God values (eg, thinking) and exalting other activities (eg, intuition) beyond even God's estimation. In the end we will be shortchanging God, ourselves and the world we live in.

### Renaissance man

God is not only keen on the development of our spirits, he is also keen on the development of the whole man. All of us is important to God. After all, he made all of us. It is not just the human spirit that has been made in the image of God, but man as a whole person. God is a Renaissance God, and he wants us to be Renaissance people. The Renaissance idealised the well-rounded individual: the man versed in art, in literature, and on the field of battle. The Bible too presents us with the ideal of whole man development.

One of the great works of art to come out of the Renaissance, a work that perhaps best embodies this ideal, was Michelangelo's statue of David (1504). This overwhelming statue is a tribute to man's beauty and greatness. Michelangelo picked well when he chose David for his subject. Who better than David lived out the Renaissance ideal. Here's how the Bible describes David: he 'knows how to play the harp. He is a brave man and a warrior. He speaks well and is a fine-looking man' (1 Sam 16:18). (Reflecting Saul's advisors' values, they add almost as an afterthought, 'And the Lord is with him.') We know in later life that David was an adept leader of men, and politically astute to boot. On top of all that he had a marvellous poetic gift. That is what I call a well-rounded individual. Usually the type of personality given to prowess in war is not given to artistic sensitivity. Nor is the imaginative artist often gifted to deal with the practical realities of government (artists please forgive me!). David was indeed the Renaissance man par excellence. And notice that God did not see this as a liability and a disqualification for spiritual service. God is not against the full development of our personalities. As a matter of fact, he used and anointed these natural gifts of David's.

If spirituality were measured by the degree we 'got out of our souls and lived out of our spirits' then the ultimate in spirituality would be death. It is at death that our spirits separate from our body. We leave our souls behind and our spirits float off (or something like that). We are then total spirit beings (see Eccles 12:7; Lk 23:46; Jas 2:26). But death is not seen as the culmination of our spiritual journey; rather it is an obstacle in it. It is our enemy, not our ideal (see 1 Cor 15:20–29).

I think we would all agree that the spiritual gifts are spiritual. Of course they are! What I am trying to say is that all the gifts of the Spirit are spiritual even though they are not just restricted to the operation of our spirit. In Romans 12:4–8 we see the gifts falling into three convenient categories:

*1. Spirit oriented*—these are the 'spiritual heavies' that need an obvious supernatural anointing in order to work. Here we could put the gifts like prophecy, teaching and leading.

*2. Soul oriented*—these are the more 'ordinary', human gifts like encouraging and showing mercy.

*3. Body oriented*—gifts that have to do with ministering to physical needs; the gifts of serving and giving.

These are all spiritual gifts. They are all 'spiritual heavies' to God. None are second-rate in his sight. The most spiritual thing to do if you meet a starving man is not to prophecy to him but feed him. Feeding the man does nothing directly for his spirit, but it is spiritual in that it is important to God and is a reflection of his heart.

So let's be done with a chopped down, anaemic version

of spirituality that would consign whole areas of man's personality to a guilt-ridden, second-class existence. It's whole man or bust. Let's use all that God has given as we seek to find and do his will. Just how we do this will be the subject of the next chapter.

# 7

# *The Ignored Art of Decision-Making*

Believing that God speaks today, we naturally ask, 'How then can we hear his voice?' Believing that reason is ordained of God we ask, 'How then can we make good decisions?' If God has entrusted responsibility to man as a rational creature, then the better the decisions man makes, the better he carries out this responsibility.

Decision-making is an inescapable part of life. It is also an ignored art. Few of us sit down and think through just what the essential elements are that make up a good decision. What makes a good decision different from a bad decision? Do we have to wait for the outcome to find out? (If it flops it was a bad decision, and if it gloriously succeeds it was a good decision?) But the whole point of decision-making is to avoid flops beforehand. It is too late, once you are married, to find out it was not a very good decision.

The often used criterion in decision-making is to list the pros and cons on any question and decide on the basis of which side outweighs the other. This approach works admirably on questions which are fairly simple and where the options are obvious. For example, if one were to decide on whether or not to swim in shark-infested waters one could make a list as follows:

| PROS | CONS |
|------|------|
| 1. It's good to feed fish. They are part of God's creation. | 1. It is better to stay alive myself. |
| | 2. One does not want to give the sharks a taste for man-meat as that would be unfair on the other swimmers and one ought, in all fairness, to consider their wishes. 'Beaches for all or not at all' is a worthy motto. |
| | 3. This beach is intended for swimming and probably does not have planning permission for shark feeding. Respect the powers that be. |

So your cons are much more heavily weighted than your pros. The result: you decide not to go swimming . . . for this day at least. Similarly, the choice of a marriage partner can at times be simplified in the same way. Just list the pros and cons:

| PROS | CONS |
|------|------|
| 1. I like her. | 1. She hates my guts. |
| 2. I am an eligible bachelor. | 2. She is already married. |
| 3. She has good teeth. | 3. She is 92 years old. |

Weighing it up the right decision soon becomes clear.

Other decisions are not so simple, and thinking in terms of pros and cons does not sufficiently focus the true issues. There are complex career choices and marriage choices which require a different approach. John Arnold and Bert Tompkins have written an excellent book called *How To Make The Right Decisions* which lays out seven steps to good decision-making. Using these steps can help you immensely.

We shall see that the apostles actually used these steps. Acts 15 is a good example of effective decision-making— and they didn't even have any management manuals! We shall also see that we instinctively and subconsciously use these steps ourselves. We do have our rules of thumb, but if we are unaware of the length of our thumbs they will be quite useless in working out measurements of a more exacting and precise nature. When we are unclear on our decision-making processes we become erratic and hit-or-miss in our approach—here a good decision, there a bad one. If we are ignorant as to what steps we took to arrive at a good decision, then we will be unable to reproduce the same process in the face of a more daunting decision. We will feel overwhelmed. While it is in the nature of finite man to be hit-and-miss, to be fallible, we want to reduce this tendency as far as is humanly possible. That is what good decision-making is all about.

Here are the steps that Arnold and Tompkins outline:
1. Determine the issues.
2. State your purpose.
3. Set up standards for evaluating alternatives.
4. Establish your priorities.
5. Search for solutions.
6. Test the alternatives.
7. Troubleshoot your decisions.

## Determine the issues

Ask yourself just why a decision has to be made. Is there really an issue demanding a decision? This is not just a device for the procrastinator of the 'do not do today what you can put off till tomorrow' ilk. It is a way of insuring that we do not fix something that is working fine, rather like children who tinker with an admirably operating mechanical device until it breaks. We have the age-old advice to 'leave well enough alone'.

Sometimes a person comes to us and pours out their difficulties and problems. Rather than instantly feeling we need to advise them on a course of action, and feeling we should make some decisions about what they should do, perhaps all that is really necessary is a listening ear. Perhaps, in fact, they would resent any proffered advice. What may be required is simply a good dose of human sympathy and warmth.

Asking 'why' and 'what' helps to clarify the issue. 'Why do I need to make a decision?' Then ask, 'What is happening that I do not want to happen? What is happening that I do want to happen?' If there are satisfactory answers to these 'why' and 'what' questions then it is highly likely that you do not have to make a decision.

Sometimes the issue is smacking us in the face and little examination of the real issues is required. If we stroll by a house ablaze and catch sight of a damsel in distress shouting for help from the window, we hardly need to take ourselves off to some quiet arbour to wrestle through, 'Now is there an issue here that I must make a decision about?'

In Acts 15 it was clear what the issue was and that some decision needed to be made about it. A deep division and dispute was being caused by some Jewish believers who came down to Antioch teaching that Gentile converts had to be circumcised. People were lining up on both sides of the argument. Emotions were running high. The old division between Gentile and Jew was being activated. Clearly, here was an issue that had to be settled.

### State your purpose

Ask yourself whether there is a bigger issue behind the immediate issue we are facing. In Acts 15 there was indeed a deeper issue underneath the question of circumcision. At one level, insisting on a physical circumcision could seem like quite a superficial matter. Was God too concerned one way or the other about a mere bodily mark? Did not the apostle Paul himself say, 'Circumcision is nothing and uncircumcision is nothing' (1 Cor 7:19)? Yet the apostles saw that underneath this quarrel about a simple physical act was the fundamental question of how a man is saved. This is why Paul was so adamant on this issue. Was Jesus' death alone, responded to by faith alone, sufficient, or did we need to add some other crucial act such as circumcision? To the challenge that 'unless you are circumcised . . . you cannot be saved' (Acts 15:1) the apostles answered that God 'purified their hearts through faith . . . it is through the grace of our Lord Jesus that we are saved, just as they are' (vv 9, 11).

At this second stage in our decision-making process we are trying to broaden out our thinking. We are trying to escape tunnel vision by looking at the deeper issues underneath the immediate decision that presents itself to us. If we do not do this we may miss the real point we will miss the real problem and narrow down our alternative solutions.

Good businesses need to think this way in order to survive in a changing world. The venetian blind was born when a company which made window shades began to regard themselves not just as a company that made shades but as a company that was in the light control business. They broadened out their purpose, or rather they broadened out their understanding of what they were all about. They began to view themselves in light of their overall purpose instead of defining themselves in terms of the immediate means (making window shades) to this end. This freed their thinking up to consider all sorts of alternative ways to control light besides the conventional method of shades. The result? The venetian blind.

We need to approach our decisions in exactly the same way. It is not only the doctrinal questions—such as in

Acts 15—which need to be examined for deeper issues. For instance, if you are thinking about going to a Bible school and have the brochures of two excellent institutions, instead of the first question being, 'Shall I go to Bible school one or Bible school two?', the first question should be, 'Why do I want to go to Bible school? What is my underlying purpose?' If the answer is that you want to grow in your relationship with the Lord, then maybe you should stay where you are and learn the lessons the Lord has for you there. You may learn more of the Lord's ways. If the answer is that you want to grow in the spiritual gifts the Lord has equipped you with, then maybe you should consider going overseas for a year to be involved in ministry there. If the answer is that you want to know your Bible better so that you can serve the Lord more effectively, then it may well be that one of these Bible schools is for you. But questioning the underlying purpose brings out these issues and helps us focus on what is actually at stake.

## Set up standards for evaluating alternatives

Isolating the real issue is only the first step in decision-making. Seeing the problem is important but it is not the same thing as finding the solution. We next need to decide on what will guide us in our decision. What standards will we set up to guide us through the variety of possible solutions? Once you have decided that your real concern is to learn more about the Bible and that you therefore want to go to a Bible school, you still have to decide which school. How will you decide this unless you have some standards in mind, some qualities you feel are important in any Bible school you might attend? Only then can you adequately compare the merits of one school against another. Perhaps you will be teaching the Bible in a primitive area where health care is important, and thus you are looking for a school that also teaches health care. That is a standard of evaluation which will eliminate some institutions straight away.

An excellent way to set up clear standards for evaluation is to ask:

1. What do you want to achieve by the decision you need to make?

2. What do you want to preserve by the decision you need to make?

3. What do you want to avoid by the decision you need to make?

Again, looking at Acts 15 we can see that this is exactly what the apostles did. They did not phrase it in terms of 'achieve', 'preserve', and 'avoid', but they were certainly approaching their problem from this angle. What were they trying to achieve? They wanted to achieve a solution to this vexing problem that would keep both the Jewish and Gentile converts happy without sacrificing any essential truths. What did they want to preserve? The fundamental truth they wanted to preserve was that Jesus died for our sins and that this death is all we need to enter into a relationship with God. They did not want to see this compromised or weakened by an insistence on circumcision as also necessary to salvation. What did they want to avoid? They wanted to avoid a split between the Gentile and Jewish converts who seemed on the verge of going their separate ways, with one group forming the circumcision denomination and the other the uncircumcision denomination.

## Establish your priorities

If you have a very full list of standards and criteria, then you will need to prioritise them. What are the really important criteria, and what are the ones that are less important? What conditions and goals must be met by your decision, and which are desirable but not mandatory? This is important as you may find that none of the alternatives to your dilemma will meet all your standards. In that case you are looking for an alternative that at least meets the standards which are most important to you. If, for instance, one of the two Bible schools you are considering does not cater for families, and this is a priority consideration to you because you are married with children, then this will help you in deciding which school is for you.

The apostles in Acts 15 had a clear set of priorities which they reached after much discussion. In order of priority they were:

1. Be faithful to the truth. Come what may, the biblical basis of salvation could not be compromised.

2. Another critical point was to abolish the previously important distinction between Jew and Gentile. As Peter said, 'He made no distinction between us and them' (v 9). The differences in cultures and practices remained, but their spiritual foundations were identical. They differed over superficialities but they agreed on fundamentals. The basic distinction was no longer whether you were Jew or Gentile but whether you were Christian or non-Christian.

3. The third priority was that they did not want to 'make it difficult for the Gentiles who are turning to God' (v 19) to become Christians. The Gentiles might think that believing in Christ meant becoming a Jew should circumcision be insisted upon. For some, this could have been an obstacle in the way of their conversion. Conversion was too important a matter to be impeded by a ceremonial question.

4. But the apostles also placed importance on the values and feelings of the Jewish Christians. This was their fourth priority. They did not discard altogether the Jewish believers' point of view. So they instructed the Gentile believers to follow certain Jewish practices ('abstain . . . from the meat of strangled animals and from blood' v 20 . . . strongly forbidden to the Jews in Leviticus

17:10, 14). This would promote harmony by showing that on non-essentials parties on both sides were prepared to give ground.

Priorities can be very personal things. There are some priorities which are the same for all Christians. These would include the moral absolutes of the Bible. The Christian is not given the scope to decide whether or not he shall put loving and worshipping God near the top of his priority list. To be a Christian means that we love and worship God. However, how we go about this is a personal matter that permits, within limits, a wide range of possibilities.

At this prioritising stage it is relevant to bring into our decision-making process the question of our gifts and callings. All other things being equal, we want to give priority to the expression of our spiritual gifts (in accordance with 1 Peter 4:10: 'Each one should use whatever gift he has received to serve others. . .'). I say all other things being equal because the Lord could well want us to broaden our experience and learn lessons outside the area of our spiritual gifts. But generally we can consider our spiritual gifts as important factors because God gave them to us to use and not just to admire.

If my spiritual gift is teaching, then one of my priorities is to find a way to use this gift. Perhaps I should not plan to build a career choice around practical work for which I have no gift. If my gift is practical serving, I should not plan a vocation that majored on teaching the Bible (unless I have a gift for that too).

On the subject of priorities we also want to stay very open to the voice of God. Perhaps as we are listing priorities the Holy Spirit will speak to us saying, 'This here is a priority to you, but I want to change your priorities. In fact, this point over here is what I consider to be a priority for your life.' The renewing of the mind that Paul speaks of in Romans 12:2 also plays a part here. As we grow as Christians and are conformed more to his

image, God's intention is that we think like him and value
what he values. This can only mean a change of priorities.
So let's stay open to God and ask him to give us his
priorities.

## Search for solutions

We need to ask what alternatives might meet the standards we have established. Ask God for creative
solutions, possibilities you have never entertained before.
Widen your thinking. Do not just focus down to the
obvious. If you are considering Bible school, do not just
stick with the two choices known to you. Get more information on others. Have you considered going abroad?
What about home study?

The church leaders in Acts 15 had several alternatives
before them. They could have abolished Jewish Christianity. That is, they could have forbidden the practice of
all Jewish rites by believers. On the other hand, they
could have abolished Gentile Christianity. They could
have insisted that all Gentiles be circumcised on the basis
that the new covenant did not break or throw out the
old covenant but fulfilled it. These alternatives did not,
however, measure up to the standards they had set.

But even within the solution they chose there were
several alternatives. They could have permitted the eating
of blood by Gentile believers while requiring them to
make a pilgrimage to Jerusalem every five years. This
certainly would have communicated respect for the Jews.
Its drawback was that it would be too expensive and
impractical for the Gentiles. One could think of all sorts
of Jewish practices to insist on, and in the hours they
discussed this vexing question all sorts of alternatives
probably flew through their heads. Refraining from blood
had the advantage of being simple and relatively painless
to the Gentiles. It is no wonder that they settled on this
as a good solution.

## Test the alternatives

We will now compare our alternatives to the criteria we have set up. We are looking for those alternatives which best meet our priorities and standards. Acts 15 is all about testing alternatives. The point of having a council was to gather church leaders with different perspectives and to have them suggest and weigh up the alternative solutions to 'the Gentile problem'.

To help you test your alternatives you may want to grade your priorities. If you have one or two simple priorities it may well be enough to put a star by them. But if you find you have a number of priorities, you may want to go further than this and number them on a scale from one to ten, with ten being top points for a big priority, and one indicating just a baby priority.

It is a good idea to write all this down. Put the issue, along with its prioritised, alternative solutions, down on paper in front of you. Writing things down can clear your head because you are not trying to keep it all up there at once. It also means that you won't forget your points, and it forces you to think clearly and fully. The quality of any decision can only be as good as the quality of the information on which it is based.

The following diagram clearly shows the steps in making a decision.

| PRIORITY CRITERIA | | ALTERNATIVES | | |
|---|---|---|---|---|
| | | **Alternative 1** | **Alternative 2** | **Alternative 3** |
| | | Insist on circumcision, full stop | No circumcision, full stop | No circumcision, but some concession to Jewish believers |
| 10 points | Not compromise truth of salvation in Jesus | Fails | Succeeds | Succeeds |
| 8 points | Promote harmony with Jewish believers | Succeeds | Fails | Succeeds |
| 9 points | Show no distinction between Jew and Gentile | Fails | Succeeds | Succeeds |
| 9 points | Make it easy for Gentiles to convert | Fails | Succeeds | Succeeds |

## Troubleshoot your decisions

The last step we need to take is to ask ourselves just what could go wrong? This is what Arnold and Tompkins call the 'art of negative thinking'. And it is biblical! The apostles did just that in Acts 15. They not only thought in terms of a solution to the original problem (circumcision) but they also thought in terms of problems arising out of this solution (getting this solution accepted).

They foresaw two possible trouble spots. Firstly, they realised that their conclusion that circumcision was unnecessary would be hard for the Jewish believers to swallow. Anticipating this difficulty, they sweetened the pill by requiring concessions on the Gentiles' part as well (v 20). Secondly, they anticipated possible difficulties in Paul's dissemination of their decree. Probably there were Jewish believers in the provinces well aware of Paul's pro-Gentile stance who would suspect the erstwhile apostle of slightly twisting and interpreting the council's decree in his favour. They overcame this by two measures. Firstly, they wrote down their decision in a letter (v 23). It is harder to distort the written word than the spoken word when it is clear that the document is original. Secondly, they sent along two Jewish believers (we know they were Jewish from their Jewish names: Judas and Barsabbas) who were leaders in the church in Jerusalem (v 22). These two would be able to vouch for everything which that said. The gift of discernment is not the same as the gift of suspicion, though it sometimes may look like the same thing!

God himself troubleshoots his decisions. When he made mankind he was ready with a plan of salvation even before man rebelled. He was not caught unprepared and in a panic when things went awry.

If we are applying to a Bible school we need to think what we will do if we are not accepted by the one of our choice. If we are planning a church picnic we need to plan in advance what we will do in case it rains on the day. Is all this an exercise in unbelief? No, it is simply a reflection of the fact that we do not know all of the Lord's mind, that we often hear him imperfectly, and that even when we have the 'what to do' right we get the 'when to do' wrong. So troubleshoot your decisions.

## Everyday decision-making

I said at the beginning of the chapter that even though these steps seem frightfully complicated when they are laid out systematically, we actually employ them in our everyday decisions. Suppose a desire for a fat, moist, American chocolate chip cookie overpowers you. What do you do? Go through your seven steps of course!

*1. Determine the issue.* The issue is clearly whether I should devour a cookie or not. Do I need to make a decision? Of course I do—I'm starving!

*2. Broaden the issue.* I now recall that I have not eaten anything for two weeks, and the real issue is not just satisfaction of my appetite but an even more fundamental one of basic nourishment. Thank goodness for this seven step model – it's really helping me now!

*3. Set up standards:*

Achieve – nourishment.

Avoid—work! I am too lazy to make a meal.

Preserve—my teeth. Maybe chocolate chip cookies are not so good here. This dilemma begins to weigh heavily upon me till, with relief, I recall my other steps of good decision-making.

*4. Establish priorities.* Grudgingly I acknowledge that nourishment is the only logical priority, but I still keep a secret place in my heart for that chocolate chip cookie.

*5. Search for alternative solutions:*

I could make a meal myself.

I could go to McDonald's.

Even better, I could send my wife to fetch a Big Mac. Now I am really beginning to think creatively.

6. *Test the alternatives:*

Have you ever tasted my cooking? (Here I am mixing step six with step seven, ie, troubleshooting.)

Perhaps the car will break down on the way to McDonald's so I need to shore up my strength with a cookie now.

7. *Troubleshoot.* Maybe a Big Mac is not much more nourishing than a chocolate chip cookie anyway.

In the end I come up with the brilliant solution that I will have one cookie now to assuage my appetite while sending my dear wife off to McDonald's to meet the more long-term need for sustenance.

We think in this way even in the face of simple questions. This seven step approach is not too complex or sophisticated for any of us. However, in facing more complex questions than 'the Crisis of the Chocolate Chip Cookie', we may feel unable to cope. We don't know how to even begin to tackle the problem. Analysing what we do intuitively will help us isolate the different steps in decision-making so that we can step-by-step apply this same approach to the bigger issues. In doing so we are going one step further towards fulfilling Paul's command: '. . . in your thinking be adults' (1 Cor 14:20).

# Part Three:

# *Creativity*

# 8

## *Creativity and Guidance*

### The miracle of creativity

Pablo Casals was a world famous cellist for a reason. Norman Cousins tells of his first meeting with the man in the following words:

> I met Pablo Casals for the first time at his home in Puerto Rico just a few weeks before his ninetieth birthday. I was fascinated by his daily routine. About 8am his lovely wife Marta would help him to start the day. His various infirmities made it difficult for him to dress himself. Judging from his difficulty in walking and from the way he held his arms, I guessed he was suffering from rheumatoid arthritis. His emphysema was evident in his laboured breathing. He came into the living room on Marta's arm. He was badly stooped. His head was pitched forward and he walked with a shuffle. His hands were swollen and his fingers were clenched.
>
> Even before going to the breakfast table, Don Pablo went to the piano—which, I learned, was a daily ritual. He arranged himself with some difficulty on the piano bench, then with discernible effort raised his swollen and clenched fingers above the keyboard.
>
> I was not prepared for the miracle that was about to happen. The fingers slowly unlocked and reached towards the keys like the buds of a plant toward the sunlight. His back straightened. He seemed to breathe more freely. Now his fingers

settled on the keys. Then came the opening bars of Bach's *Wohltemperierte Klavier*, played with great sensitivity and control. I had forgotten that Don Pablo had achieved proficiency on several musical instruments before he took up the cello. He hummed as he played, then said that Bach spoke to him here—and he placed his hand over his heart.

Then he plunged into a Brahms concerto and his fingers, now agile and powerful, raced across the keyboard with dazzling speed. His entire body seemed fused with the music; it was no longer stiff and shrunken but supple and graceful and completely freed of its arthritic coils.

Having finished the piece, he stood up by himself, far straighter and taller than when he had come into the room. He walked to the breakfast table with no trace of a shuffle, ate heartily, talked animatedly, finished the meal, then went for a walk on the beach.

After an hour or so, he came back to the house and worked on his correspondence until lunch. Then he napped. When he rose, the stoop and the shuffle and the clenched hands were back again. On this particular day, a camera and recording crew from public television were scheduled to arrive in mid-afternoon. Anticipating the visit, Don Pablo said he wished some way could be found to call it off; he didn't feel up to the exertion of the filming, with its innumerable and inexplicable retakes and the extreme heat of the bright lights.

Marta, having been through these reluctances before, reassured Don Pablo, saying she was certain he would be stimulated by the meeting. She reminded him that he liked the young people who did the last filming, and that they would probably be back again. In particular, she called his attention to the lovely young lady who directed the recording.

Don Pablo brightened. 'Yes, of course,' he said, 'it will be good to see them again.'

As before, he stretched his arms in front of him and extended his fingers. Then the spine straightened and he stood up and went to his cello. He began to play. His fingers, hands, and arms were in sublime co-ordination as they responded to the demands of his brain for the controlled beauty of movement and tone. Any cellist thirty years his junior would have been proud to have such extraordinary physical command.

Twice in one day I had seen the miracle. A man almost ninety, beset with the infirmities of old age, was able to cast off his afflictions, at least temporarily, because he knew he had something of overriding importance to do. There was no mystery about the way it worked, for it happened every day. Creativity for Pablo Casals was the source of his own cortisone.[18]

Creativity was key to a man like Casals, but does creativity play a part in receiving guidance? Is creativity and guidance a contradiction in terms? Can you mix guidance (God showing us his ways) with creativity (man dreaming up his own way)? One more question: should we equate spirituality with passivity? Is the biblical ideal man squashing his own ideas and waiting passively for God to fill his mind? Is this what it means to 'let go and let God'?

It would be strange indeed if the creative God, upon making man in his own image, then proceeded to stifle and disallow the very creative urge he had put within man. In fact, when reading Genesis 1 and 2 we see that this was not God's intention in the least. God made man to be like God—'in our image, in our likeness' (Gen 1:26)—and the result was that within certain limits he was to act like God. Immediately after God made man he charged him with two duties that were reflections of God's own being: rulership and creativity. Genesis 1 and 2 actually focuses more on these activities than on man's moral responsibilities. That's how important God thought this area was.

God delegated to man the responsibility to look after and develop the earth: 'let them rule . . . over all the earth . . . fill the earth and subdue it' (Gen 1:26–28). This was not a bogus responsibility. Man was not just a puppet on the throne with God pulling all the shots behind the scenes. The picture is much more that God just left man to it. Man was to exercise his own creativity and develop

the garden as he wanted to. Man was to think up his own
names for the animals. 'He (God) brought them (the
animals) to the man to see what he would name them;
and whatever the man called each living creature, that
was its name' (Gen 2:19). God was fascinated with what
names man would concoct for his creatures. He was interested. He wanted 'to see what he (man) would name
them' (Gen 2:19). Far from slapping down man's creative
abilities, God was actively encouraging them. And man
responded with a fantastic assortment of names. When
God gave names they were simplicity itself; 'Adam' or
'Eve' suited him fine. Not man. He had never done this
sort of thing before (he literally had not had the time),
and so at the first opportunity his imagination ran riot. A
feast of tongue-twisting and mind-boggling multi-syllabic
names poured forth. The unheard of sound of orangutan
and rhinoceros was sprung upon an unsuspecting world.
Perhaps God just looked on with a shrug and thought,
'Why not?'

Creativity was written into the very nature of man. It
makes man like God, and it sets man off from the animals.
An animal acts out of instinct, not out of a creative
imagination. We will never find a beaver thinking, 'I sure
am sick of water. Water, water everywhere, and too many
drops to drink. I think I'll build myself a holiday home
on a hill and get away from it all.' For millennia beavers
have been building exactly the same sorts of houses on
water. And no animal known to man has grown impatient
with the inclement weather of its habitat and gone on to
develop central heating. But man, the image-bearer, has
done exactly that.

## Man, the imaginative ruler

Indeed, it would have been impossible for man to exercise
his God-given ruling mandate without the ability to think
creatively. Ruling over the earth was not just a matter of

'doing' but of 'thinking'. The animals could do, but they could not think; at least, they could not think imaginatively. It was man's thinking ability which fitted him to rule over the animals. The animals' 'doing' ability far outshone man. They could fly, run like the wind and lift enormous weights. But God had equipped man with imagination, and this qualified him to rule these animals and all the earth.

Science and technology, which are the means man uses to subdue the earth, are creations of man's imagination. Through science man is able to extend himself beyond his natural limitations and fly like the birds, reach speeds exceeding even the swiftest cheetah, and lift weights heavier than any elephant could possibly cope with. Scientific advance is not simply a matter of computer-like minds mechanically sifting through data and then coming to the logical conclusion which any computer would come to. Imagination is necessary.

W I Beveridge, in his book *The Art of Scientific Investigation*, explains that science has not advanced through the work of sceptical scientists who let facts speak for themselves. Facts *do not* speak for themselves! It is man who interprets them and hears them saying something. Beveridge quotes Einstein as saying, 'There is no logical way to the discovery of these elemental laws. There is only the way of intuition, which is helped by a feeling for the order lying behind the appearance.'[19] Beveridge goes on to say, 'Reason based on knowledge is usually sufficient in everyday affairs and in straightforward matters in science, but in research there is often insufficient information available for effective reasoning. Here one has to fall back on "feelings" or "taste".'[20] Feelings? Taste? Intuition? This is hardly our usual image of what science is all about.

Developing this point, Beveridge says,

In research, an attitude of mind is required for discovery

which is different from that required for proof, for discovery and proof are distinct processes.[21]

The methods and functions of discovery and proof in research are as different as are those of a detective and of a judge in a court of law. While playing the part of the detective the investigator follows clues but having captured his alleged fact, he turns judge and examines the case by means of logically arranged evidence. Both functions are equally essential but they are different.[22]

The role of reason in research is not so much in exploring the frontiers of knowledge as in developing the findings of the explorers.[23]

Imagination is key to exercising our God-ordained role of ruling and subduing the earth. Imagination has to do with creating new concepts, of dreaming up new ideas. We are creating even as God created (though he created out of nothing). Imagination is not revelation. Revelation is God speaking. Imagination is man thinking. It is a natural ability. And God gave it to man with the intention that he should use it.

## Empty channel theory

There is an 'empty channel theory' of spirituality which sees good only in that which is 'all of God and not of man'. It sees any mixture of man's thoughts and desires as impurity that discolours God's pure will. Man's thoughts are seen as the fly in the ointment the minerals which build up inside a water pipe gradually choking out the supply of clear water. Clear out this build-up and you will get God's unimpeded supply.

But this view is totally at odds with God's intentions as laid out in Genesis 1 and 2. God wants to work with man, not just through man. The problem is not the 'self' but selfishness. God made our individual selves. He does not want to obliterate them. Just why God wants to work with man is a mystery. If God put priority on perfection, on excellence alone, then he would definitely work *through* man rather than *with* man. The empty channel model would be the far superior one. The contributions of finite man cannot compete with the contributions of an infinite, perfect God.

But on this view, not only would man be redundant in the universe, the angels themselves would find themselves unemployed. Even they could not compare with the quality of God's work. But God is not solely interested in perfect performance. Surely our heavenly Father views us exactly as an earthly parent does his child. The mother can do the dishes much better than the four-year-old daughter, but for the joy of the relationship she lets her take part. The dishes take longer, the floor now needs to be cleaned up as well, but the relationship is enriched and the child learns. In this way, God includes us in on his plans.

## Freedom principle

God's intention was to give man freedom of choice within certain boundaries. Even before there was sin in the world the ideal was not that God was to tell man every little thing. We note in Genesis 2:16 that God's order was 'You are free to eat from any tree. . .' rather than, 'You can eat from this tree on Monday, that one on Tuesday, the south-east corner of the orchard on Wednesday. . . .'

God has not totally changed in his dealings with man since the Fall. This 'freedom principle' is found throughout the Bible. It is even part of the Jews' meticulously ordered ceremonial rites. The same God who forbade any freedom of choice in certain areas, warning Moses 'when he was about to build the tabernacle: "See to it that you make everything according to the pattern shown you on the mountain" ' (Heb 8:5), also said the following:

'You may eat any animal that has a split hoof . . . and that chews the cud' (Lev 11:3). Here we see the freedom principle in operation. Just as Adam and Eve had a wide range of fruit from which to choose, so the Jews had a wide range of meat from which they could freely choose.

'If a man or woman wants to make a special vow, a vow of separation to the Lord as a Nazirite. . .' (Num 6:2). This vow was something you did of your own free will. God said 'if'. God did not require anyone to take on this lifestyle, but for those who wanted to he gave them the opportunity.

'If any of you . . . presents a gift for a burnt offering . . . as a freewill offering. . .' (Lev 22:18). Notice the 'if' again. The 'if' indicates that this particular offering is not a required one. That is what makes it a 'freewill' offering. And the Jews could pick whether they offered a bull, a ram or a goat. Freedom within limits.

Today we still have freedom within limits. Certain sincere Christians say that because something is not specifically mentioned in Scripture we cannot use it. So no electric guitars—or electric lights, for that matter! Francis Schaeffer writes:

> It is my thesis that as we cannot bind men morally except with that which the Scriptures clearly command (beyond that we can only give advice), similarly, anything the New Testament does not command in regard to church form is a freedom to be exercised under the leadership of the Holy Spirit for that particular time and place. . . . It seems clear to me that the opposite cannot be held, namely that only that which is commanded is allowed. If this were the case, then, for example, to have a church building would be wrong and so would having church bells or a pulpit, using books for singing, following any specific order of service, standing to sing, and many other like things.[24]

## Freedom in the biggies?

We can grant that there is freedom in the smaller decisions, in the ceremonial areas of life. Does this freedom principle still apply to the big decisions in life? Let me answer with a clear 'Yes and no'. Sometimes it does, and sometimes it doesn't. Let's look at some major decisions in the Bible where man's own initiative and creativity did play a part in doing the will of God.

In 1 Samuel 14 is chronicled the exploits of Jonathan, son of Saul. The Israelites are at war with the Philistines, and Jonathan is wondering what the will of God is— should he go up and fight them? Notice how he approaches this situation: 'Come, let's go over to the outpost of those uncircumcised fellows. Perhaps the Lord will act on our behalf . . . if they say, "Come up to us," we will climb up, because that will be our sign that the Lord has given them into our hands' (1 Sam 14:6–10). Jonathan is not sure of what the Lord's will is—he says 'perhaps the Lord will act'—but what he does not do is just sit and wait passively. He takes the initiative himself by engaging the enemy. He moved out in the right general direction, in what he knew to be the general will of God. He knew that Saul was the God-ordained king (1 Sam 9:15–17) and that God wanted to deliver his people from the Philistines (1 Sam 9:16). He takes steps, but only very tentative ones until he is clearer on God's particular design in this instance. Jonathan wants to do God's will, and this means co-operation between God and himself. He takes initiative, but within limits.

And look too at 2 Samuel 7 where we read of King David wanting to do something for God. He is unhappy living in a splendid palace while God's 'house' is a comparatively shabby tent. So he has an idea: why not build God a magnificent temple? David tells the prophet Nathan what he has on his mind. God responds through Nathan in three ways.

He is thrilled to bits with David's heart attitude. That is plain from the way he heaps promises back on David, so many promises that David just sits down stunned (v 18ff). It's as if God is saying, 'You want to bless me; well I want to bless you.'

God then asks an interesting question, saying, '. . . did I ever say to any of their rulers whom I commanded to shepherd my people Israel, "Why have you not built me a house of cedar?" ' (2 Sam 7:7). That is to say, God had never ordered a temple to be built. The Old Testament prophesied that God would choose one specific location in Israel for the tabernacle, but that location was for the tent. In other words, the building of a temple *was David's idea, not God's!* Think about that! God was saying that he was quite happy in a tent, thank you (after all, who is impressed with a house of gold when you have heaven?), but if David wants to build a temple, well, go ahead. We are seeing here what it means to be 'God's fellow workers' (2 Cor 6:1). We are joined with God in a partnership, a partnership of creativity. We not only work with God in our doing but in our thinking, in our imagining.

God's last response to David was to tell him, 'Yes, but. . . .' God said 'yes' to David's idea of a temple, but 'no' to David being the builder. God used David's idea, but he pruned it first. The Lord is not automatically obliged to accept man's wonderful, creative ideas. It would seem to go without saying that the Lord is still the Lord. But I have said it anyway because things that go without saying often don't get said . . . and that hardly seems right.

Some would draw the wrong lesson from Moses' incident in Exodus 2:11ff where he kills an Egyptian. Acts 7:25 shows that Moses thought he was doing the will of God and that this would be the beginning of God's deliverance for his people. He was wrong. Instead of deliverance he spent the next forty years in exile communing with sheep. The lesson here is not that Moses erred in taking the initiative for God. Rather, his error was that he took initiative without any consultations with God whatsoever. Unlike David and Jonathan he just acted, as the politicians says, unilaterally. How different was his second attempt forty years later.

Man was meant to dream and scheme, to take initiative. God wants independent thinkers with dependent spirits. We are meant to co-operate with God in it all. We need to ask God what his thoughts are. In response, God will sometimes say 'no' to our request, as he did when Jesus asked, 'My Father, if it is possible, may this cup be taken from me' (Mt 26:39). Sometimes he will say 'yes' as he did with Jonathan. And at other times he will say 'yes, but . . .' as he did to King David.

Man has a significant part to play in doing the will of God. Incredibly, his significant part is not just in doing God's will but in the actual forming of what it is. We so often ask God, 'What do you want me to do for you?' God sometimes asks us in return, 'What do you want me to do for you?' (Mt 20:32). God is saying, 'Come on man, play your part.' Partners work together and both contribute. The senior partner has the final say but not the sole say.

We can make sense of a scripture like John 2:1–11 when we understand that God makes room for our own thinking and initiative. When Mary first told Jesus that there was no more wine at the wedding feast, his immediate response was, 'Dear woman, why do you involve me? My time has not yet come' (Jn 2:4). That's that, one would think. But no, a short time later Jesus was at work; and what was he doing? He was turning water into wine! But I thought his time for this sort of thing had not come! What is happening here? Is the key to understanding this turn of events found in Jesus' super-sensitivity to the minute timing of God? That is, 2:55pm was not water-turning time but 3:15pm was? I think not. Jesus would not have corrected Mary for being twenty minutes out on her timing. If exact timing was the issue here then I would say that Mary was fairly accurate; she got the right day (not bad, out of thirty years), but just not the right minute.

I do not think it was a question of precise on-the-minute timing. I think that Jesus was saying that his miraculous ministry was not to start for a few more days or weeks and that he was not intending on doing any miracles at the wedding feast. But all that changed when Mary involved herself. She did not take 'no' for an answer. (Mums haven't changed over 2,000 years!) Graciously, Jesus did not give 'no' for a reply. In response to the pleas of his mother he brought his timing forward and began his miraculous ministry then and there. Amazing!

There is no such thing as Christian fatalism. Fatalism is not the intended consequence of the doctrine that God rules the earth and guides man. 'Que sera, sera,' is not the Christian's motto. 'What will be, will be,' may be well and good for other religions but not for the Christian. He is called to rule the earth as God's fellow-worker. He is to participate and contribute. He is to step out under God and exercise himself as the image-bearer of God. And as he does this he will have the thrill of participating in a glorious adventure with God.

## Scripture writers—inspired zombies or creative inventors?

God loves creativity and encourages it in his servants. But does this view of guidance have dangerous implications for the absolute inspiration of Scripture? If the originators of Holy Writ were led by a combination of divine guidance and human creativity are we left with an unreliable Bible which is partly of man and therefore not wholly of God? Does the humanity of the authors of Scripture interfere with their inspiration?

Succinctly: no! The 'empty channel theory' falls again! We can believe totally in inspiration without the need to say that God obliterated the personality of Peter and Paul in the act of inspiration. They did not turn into zombies upon picking up their quill pens. God used their personalities. See how action-oriented Peter's letters are, almost totally concerned with practical advice on how to live the Christian life, whereas theologically trained Paul devotes much more space to issues of theology and principles underlying our actions (seventy-five per cent of Romans, for instance, covers theological principles). The apostle Peter, ever straightforward in his thinking, even admitted that he found some of Paul's theological letters 'hard to understand'. (See 2 Peter 3:16. Note too that, in mentioning 'the other Scriptures', Peter is classing Paul's writings as Scripture.)

God not only used the personalities of the writers of Scripture, but their personal experiences and circumstances as well. Think of the Psalms which are almost entirely emotive outbursts occasioned by some real life experience, good and bad. But this does not detract from their inspiration. Jesus himself, in Mark 12:36, quotes David's Psalm 110:1, attributing it not to David's genius but to the Holy Spirit's genius: 'David himself, *speaking by the Holy Spirit*. . .' (my emphasis added).

Psalm 110 is obviously a prophetic utterance. Some of the other psalms can seem much more ordinary, reflecting the highs and lows of human experience, but the witness of Scripture is that they are equally inspired. While allowing the human element to remain, God insured that the divine element stood pre-eminent. Note how the New Testament writers regarded these Psalms:

| *Old Testament Designation:* | | *New Testament Designation:* | |
|---|---|---|---|
| The psalmist said | (Ps 95:7) | The Holy Spirit says | (Heb 3:7) |
| The psalmist said | (Ps 45:6) | God said | (Heb 1:8) |
| The psalmist said | (Ps 102:25–27) | God said | (Heb 1:1–10) |

The incredible fact is that it was God who was working in and through these writers as they recorded their observations and insights. In their speaking God was speaking! Therefore, as we read the Bible we are reading more than just the words of spiritual men who are doing their best to share their insights with us. We are reading more than just the words of sages who are trying to understand God 'as far as is humanly possible'. We are reading the 'very words of God' (Rom 3:2). This means that God saw to it that the writers' personalities and experiences did not discolour what they wrote. He insured that what they wrote was wholly true and therefore wholly dependable. A Bible mixed with human errors could hardly be called the 'very words of God' as he is a God who does not lie and does not err.

While leaving room for the human element in Scripture, we must never underplay the divine element. Without it we have no Scripture! One of the differences between Scripture and current prophecy is that in Scripture the human never swallowed up or overshadowed the divine, while in modern prophecy this not infrequently happens. Modern prophecy is not inerrant and can easily contain that which is of purely human origin as well as that which is of divine origin (ie, it can be wrong).

The doctrine of biblical inspiration is as pivotal to Christianity as is the doctrine of the divinity of Christ. The same one who said, 'I and the Father are one' (Jn 10:30), said, 'Scripture cannot be broken' (Jn 10:35). Jesus, who claimed the right to rule over all men and all creation, still submitted his life work and direction to the rule of Scripture, saying over and over again, 'That which is written must be fulfilled.' Jesus had a high view of Scripture, believing, as the apostle Paul did, that 'All Scripture is God-breathed' (2 Tim 3:16).

To an unbelieving world this doctrine of biblical inspiration is a scandal. Worse, its intellectual credibility is regarded as so lightweight that calling it a scandal grants

it unbefitting dignity. Most would simply dismiss it as a
bad joke. I well remember a friend of mine asking me,
'You don't really believe the Bible is the literal word of
God, do you?' The note of rising incredulity would not
have been greater if I had said I believed in a flat earth.

Christians, who were told by their Master, 'If the world
hates you, keep in mind that it hated me first' (Jn 15:18),
should, of course, be prepared for this sort of mild opposition. Conflict is the natural result of our faith meeting
the world's faith (in man, technology, education, or whatever fad is the flavour of the month). But understand that
the conflict is between faith and faith, not, as the debate
is so often posed, between faith and reason. (Both faith
and reason are necessary. I decry both unreasonable faith
and faithless reason but, given the choice, give me
unreasonable faith any day. It's unreasonable faith which
will keep me going to the end of a punishing marathon,
to the top of an 'impossible' mountain, and to a home in
a heaven above.)

The religious sceptic cannot prove that God doesn't
exist, that God is not personal, and that God never speaks
to men. He simply 'believes' these things. The Christian,
believing in an all-powerful and personal God, does not
find it unreasonable that this God can and does speak and
that he does his speaking in the Bible.

The apostle Paul wrote, '. . . if the trumpet does not
sound a clear call, who will get ready for battle?' (1 Cor
14:8). If our Bible is merely the work of men its only
contribution is a weak and windy 'Phhht'. It would be as
useful as a life raft full of holes. But it is not simply the
work of men. It is the blast of God summoning us to his
call. It is full of truth, free from error, and full of God.

# 9

# *Guidance Stew*

Perhaps you have reached this point thinking, 'If finding God's will is this complicated, then I quit.' Well, rest assured . . . it's going to get worse! Just joking, just joking. But it does seem complicated when we hear that sometimes we can make our own decision and sometimes God wants to direct us himself; when we have to be open to the ten different ways God can speak, while at the same time not forgetting to fulfil the five conditions for hearing his voice. It is no wonder that Paul's prayer for the Colossian believers went like this: '. . . we have not stopped praying for you and asking God to fill you with the knowledge of his will through all spiritual wisdom and understanding' (Col 1:9). It was evidently not always an easy thing to know the will of God. It took much prayer and it took wisdom.

Thankfully guidance, though having many aspects to consider and ways of going about it, boils down to one simple thing: walking with Jesus and looking to him to fulfil his promise that 'the Spirit of truth . . . will guide you into all truth' (Jn 16:13). Guidance is simple in the doing but complicated in the analysis. In this it is no different than the rest of life. Take walking, for instance. If we were to analyse all the varied muscular contractions that needed to be co-ordinated, we would consider walking a feat on the same plane as landing a man on the moon. Yet we do it every day, not because it is not complicated (any baby can tell you otherwise) but because we have mastered the complicated and have made it simple.

The apostle Paul sees that we need wisdom in our pursuit of guidance. We need wisdom in combining God's way of guidance through listening to the voice of God, through using our God-given gift of reason, and through our own initiative and imagination. How do we put these together? We need wisdom here as God has not seen it fitting to give us a definitive rule book covering all the types of decisions we will face in life and which mode of guidance is appropriate to each type of decision. Life is not neatly compartmentalised like that. Rather, all these elements must be mixed together in a kind of guidance stew. How to mix them so we have a nice stew rather than an experiment that has gone wrong takes wisdom. Wisdom is not just knowledge. It is knowledge plus judgement. In regard to guidance, wisdom is not just knowing the ten ways God speaks or the five conditions, but wisdom is knowing how to apply this knowledge to our lives. Knowing God's will is not just a matter of applying a pat formula that delivers guaranteed results. Pat formulas leave out one consideration: God is alive. ('Ah, yes. I forgot about that.') God is a personal being, not an answering box. Guidance is not a matter of pressing the right button and—bingo—out comes the appropriate reply. The wisdom we need in guidance comes not from rules but from relationship—our relationship with God.

The earlier chapters gave an overview on guidance and avoided excursions into particulars. We did not get down to how this overall view could specifically help us in areas where we so feel the need for guidance—for instance, what career to pursue and who we should marry. I have been constructing a building, putting up the overall structure, but, as yet, I have not filled up any of the rooms.

We need to do this. If we want to construct a home to dwell in then we not only want the overall structure put up but the individual rooms kitted out. In this chapter we want to look at how we might move from our overall structure—the broad principles of guidance—into one of the 'rooms' of life in which we invest much time and concern: vocation.

## Vocation

How do we know what our vocation/job/ministry should be? How do we know whether we should be a preacher, a social worker, a politician, or a painter/decorator? Vocation is not a word we use much today. It is a word that denotes calling, or ministry. In normal usage it has slightly broader overtones than the word 'ministry' in that ministry usually calls up pictures of preachers, counsellors, miracle workers, and so on (sometimes known as 'the five-fold ministry' of Ephesians 4:11). 'Vocation' has a connotation which covers all of life, sacred and secular (though really, ministry and vocation are one and the same thing.). Vocation communicates that there is a slot in life suited just for us that God has given to us. It is the sense Paul communicates in 1 Corinthians 7:17 where he says, 'Nevertheless, each one should retain the place in life that the Lord assigned to him and to which God has called him.'

If we were making a career choice and deciding on taking a job, we would want to apply the four guidelines mentioned in the first chapter of this book;

1. The Bible   Is it a profession that the Bible allows or forbids?
2. The Spirit   What is the Holy Spirit telling us?
3. My own judgement   What do I think of it?
4. My own initiative   What would I like to do?

After going through steps one and two you may not even need to go on to steps three and four. Perhaps God has spoken to you so clearly through the Bible and by his Spirit that his will is obvious to you. Terrific. However, it is not always this clear. If this is the case it is helpful, as you continue to seek God in prayer, to go on to steps three and four.

Steps one and two are self-explanatory, but steps three and four need further clarification. It is not enough to say, 'Make a judgement.' We need to know how to make a good judgement. And though our seven steps in Chapter 7 give us an overall approach, they are too general. These seven steps are like computer hardware—they give you the machinery to enable you to solve many problems, but only when you have fed in the software. We still need to feed in guidelines for our decision-making. What biblical guidelines and standards are there which can guide us in our job choices?

As we make vocational choices we need to ask three more questions:

1. What am I looking for in a job?
2. What are my abilities?
3. What are my desires?

We need to know what we are looking for in a job. Are we looking for a job in which to express the ministry God has given us, or are we looking for a job that will primarily be a source of financial support. A job-as-ministry will probably greatly narrow down our possible choices, whereas a job-as-support increases our choices considerably. Job-as-ministry and job-as-support are not mutually contradictory, but they are different. It is important to know which we are looking for in a job as jobs will meet the 'support' criteria but not all jobs will give us the opportunity to exercise our spiritual gifts. If our spiritual gift is teaching then in all likelihood being a bricklayer is not the job to take to open up this ministry. It will do great, though, for meeting the 'support' criteria.

Let's be clear that both are valid considerations. It is not wrong to look for a job that primarily is a means to bring in money. More than not being wrong, it is a biblical priority.

> We were not idle when we were with you, nor did we eat anyone's food without paying for it. On the contrary, we worked night and day, labouring and toiling so that we would not be a burden to any of you . . . we gave you this rule: 'If a man will not work, he shall not eat.' We hear that some among you are idle. . . . Such people we command . . . to settle down and earn the bread they eat (2 Thess 3:7–12).

> If anyone does not provide for his relatives, and especially for his immediate family, he has denied the faith and is worse than an unbeliever (1 Tim 5:8). (Strong words!)

Equally, it is not only valid to seek an outlet for our ministry, it is commanded in Scripture. 'Serve the Lord,' the Bible says. The Greek word 'diakoneo', which we translate 'to minister', can equally be translated 'to serve' (and indeed *is* in verses like Luke 12:37). We serve the Lord by exercising our ministry which consists mainly in the use of our spiritual gifts.

There are three basic models for relating our jobs to our ministries. They are:

1. *Job as mainly support and partly ministry.* One's ministry consists mainly in openings outside the job in places such as one's home group, specially organised ministry trips abroad, and prison or hospital visiting. Even in this model there is still 'ministry' going on at the job. Anyone in a job is involved in the ministry of being salt and light to a dark world—plus one is involved in the ministry of giving as one practises tithing one's income to the Lord's work (or just giving if one does not practise rigid tithing).

2. *Job as equally support and equally ministry.* Ministry opportunities outside the job are an extra bonus but not vital to opening up ministry, as one's ministry is mainly on the job anyway. This job could be a religious job like a

pastor who gets paid for his work, or it could be someone engaged in secular work. An architect friend of mine sees his work not only as a means of support but as a way to build the kingdom. He not only sets aside a portion of his profits to help Christian projects in the third world, but he has also gone into partnership with others of like mind to enable him to take one to two months of the year off. This allows him to go to the third world to help with various architectural projects.

Norman Vincent Peale tells the story of Ralston Young, redcap number 42 in the Grand Central Station in New York.

He carries bags for a living, but his real job is living the spirit of Christ as a redcap in one of the world's greatest railway stations. As he carries a man's suitcase, he tries to share a little Christian fellowship with him. He carefully watches a customer to see if there is any way in which he can give him more courage and hope. He is very skilful in the way he goes about it too.

One day, for example, he was asked to take a little old lady to her train. She was in a wheelchair, so he took her down on the elevator. As he wheeled her into the elevator he noticed that there were tears in her eyes. Ralston Young stood there as the elevator descended, closed his eyes, and asked the Lord how he could help her, and the Lord gave him an idea. As he wheeled her off the elevator, he said with a smile, 'Ma'am, if you don't mind me saying so, that is a mighty pretty hat you are wearing.'

She looked up at him and said, 'Thank you.'

'And I might add,' he said, 'that sure is a pretty dress you have on. I like it so much.'

Being a woman, this appealed to her, and despite the fact that she was not feeling well, she brightened up and asked, 'Why in the world did you say those nice things to me? It is very thoughtful of you.'

'Well,' he said, 'I saw how unhappy you were. I saw that you were crying and I just asked the Lord how I could help you. The Lord said, "Speak to her about her hat." The mention of the dress,' he added, 'was my own idea.' Ralston Young and the Lord together knew how to get a woman's mind off her troubles.

'Don't you feel well?' he then asked.

'No,' she replied, 'I am constantly in pain. I am never free from it. Sometimes I think I can't stand it. Do you, by any chance, know what it means to be in pain all the time?'

Ralston had an answer, 'Yes, ma'am, I do, for I lost an eye, and it hurt like a hot iron day and night.'

'But,' she said, 'you seem to be happy now. How did you accomplish it?'

By this time he had her in her seat in the train, and he said, 'Just by prayer, ma'am, just by prayer.'

Softly she asked, 'Does prayer, just prayer, take your pain away?'

'Well,' answered Ralston, 'perhaps it doesn't always take it away. I can't say that it does, but it always helps to overcome it so it doesn't seem like it hurts so much. Just keep on prayin', ma'am, and I'll pray for you too.'

Her tears were dried now, and she looked up at him with a lovely smile, took him by the hand, and said, 'You've done me so much good.'

A year passed, and one night in Grand Central Station Ralston Young was paged to come to the Information booth. A young woman was there who said, 'I bring you a message from the dead. Before she died my mother told me to find you and to tell you how much you helped her last year when you took her to the train in her wheelchair. She will always remember you, even in eternity. She will always remember you, for you were so kind and loving and understanding.'[25]

That is practising a ministry—a ministry of encouragement and service on the job. It's wonderfully possible.

3. *Our third model of relating job to ministry is having no supporting job and spending most of one's time in one's ministry*. In this category we would place full-time Christian workers who receive no salary. Jesus, after spending most of his life in category one, spent the last three years of his life in this third category.

When we are looking for a career we need to know what we are looking for—support or ministry, or somewhere in between. If we are mainly considering a job as support then it is not so important to find a job that is in line with our spiritual gifts. If, on the other hand, we feel it is quite important that our jobs be a main avenue for the expression of our ministry then it will be quite important that it gives scope for the expression of our spiritual gifts.

Whether we are to seek job-as-support or job-as-ministry is totally up to God's individual leading in our lives. There is no rule we can use saying this or that personality type should go into 'full-time Christian work', or that medium-commitment Christians should stick to 'job-as-support but maximum-commitment Christians can launch into job-as-ministry. We see twelve and then seventy-two disciples launched into full-time Christian work in Jesus' day, with the majority staying where they were—people like rich Joseph of Arimathea who followed Jesus but continued in his previous career.

All important, however, if you are in the job-as-support category, is that you are thinking in terms of ministry. Security and provision are not sufficient motivation for the Christian life. What else could Jesus have meant when he said, 'So do not worry, saying, "What shall we eat?" or "What shall we drink?" or "What shall we wear?" For the pagans run after all these things. . . . But seek first his kingdom. . .' (Mt 6:31–33). If our ministry is not on the job then our job as Christians is to be actively involved in exploring where our ministry is to be found. Otherwise, Jesus says that we will be no different than the pagans in our lifestyles. Not much of a recommendation for a Christian!

## Gift theology

So ask first what you are seeking in a job—ministry or
support. How do we know what our ministry is? God calls
us, certainly, but what if we are not clear on what the
Lord is saying to us? The approach labelled 'gift theology'
by C Peter Wagner says that we can hear God's call
through our spiritual gifts. God has not given us these
gifts just so we can store them away proudly. He has
given us these gifts to use. If God wants us to use these
gifts then we immediately have a good guide as to what
our ministry area should be.

Wagner contrasts 'gift theology' with 'consecration
theology'. Consecration theology teaches that the secret
to receiving guidance is deeper and deeper levels of consecration to God. The teaching goes that the more we give
up our will to do the will of God the more readily will he
then reveal his will. Now this is true of course, but there
is more to guidance than that. God has given us some
very practical, concrete indicators of the general direction
he would have us go, such as our gifts.

We see Paul in Romans 12:1–8 teaching both these
theologies. Paul reminds the Romans of God's wonderful
promise that they will 'be able to test and approve what
God's will is—his good, pleasing and perfect will' (v 2).
He not only gives the promise but shows how we can
know this perfect will of God. He says the foundation is
not conforming to the pattern of this world but
wholeheartedly offering our bodies to God as living sacrifices (vv 1–2, consecration theology). He then goes on to
tell them how they should think of themselves (vv 3–8).
In doing so he covers two aspects: 1) attitude—it should
be one of humility and not of pride (v 3); and 2)
function—they need to know their function, to see where
they fit into the body of Christ, and this they can tell by
what gifts they have been given (v 4ff).

Paul has been talking in Romans 12:1–2 about how to

know ('test and approve') the will of God. Paul moves from discussing the need for consecration to the need for being aware of one's gifts: 'We have different gifts. . . . If a man's gift is prophesying, let him use it. . .' (v 6). In other words, 'Do you wonder what God's good, pleasing and perfect will for you is? Then look at the gifts he has given you and use them. That is his will.'

This is the reason Paul says, '. . . think of yourself with sober judgement' (v 3). See where your gifts really are and be content with that. Don't have an unrealistic picture of yourself. Drunkenness distorts the senses; sobriety keeps the head clear and perceptions accurate. Don't look at yourself through the magnifying glass of pride or the warped lenses of insecurity. See what God has put in you and use it. That is his will.

Gifts are good indicators of the direction in which our ministry lies. What happens if we feel that our ministry should be in a certain area but as yet we do not see the necessary gifts for it? Let's say you feel you should be teaching the Bible but you find it difficult to study; as a matter of fact you cannot even read! What then? I would say that it is valid to entertain entering a ministry in which one does not, at the beginning, display any gifting. However, in the end, a manifest gift will be the ultimate confirmation that this sense of call is right. Spiritual gifts are just spiritual equipment needed to get the job done. And God does not appoint someone to a job and then not equip them. He is not a sergeant who gives you a toothbrush with the instructions to sweep out the regimental barracks. If he really has called us to a job it will be evident in the gifts he gives us. So if we feel called to a certain area in which we show no gifting then the best thing we can do is to test out this call by taking tentative steps in the direction we feel, begin to get training and experience in that area (training will not put ability into us; it will not put a spiritual gift into us that is not there, but it will develop what is there already), and see if this gift begins to be stirred up within us. If not, it would seem wise to abandon that direction.

To take up a ministry one must not only display a willingness but an ability. Attitude and aptitude are equally important. Right through the Bible gifts and abilities are used as a guide to a person's place, to their spiritual job description. Skills are not ignored. In 1 Chronicles 15:22 we read that 'Kenaniah the head Levite was in charge of the singing; that was his responsibility. . .' What was this job based on? Not on his position as chief Levite but 'because he was skilful at it.' King David himself was anointed as an unproved boy to the office of king in Israel. When the prophet Samuel did this he was told not to judge on the basis of the outer appearance of the heir elect because 'Man looks at the outward appearance, but the Lord looks at the heart' (1 Sam 16:7). This does not mean that David showed no gifts for leading a nation, but just that as a developing teenager his physical appearance was not very impressive. Indeed, he had already shown plenty of courage, judgement and coolness of mind when as a shepherd he had taken on a lion and a bear and won (1 Sam 17:34–36). He had already been displaying traits that would be necessary in a king, but only God had seen them.

Where the Spirit leads us he gifts us. Where he has not gifted us he is not leading us. Parcelling out spiritual abilities has always been central to the Spirit's ministry. The very first time the Bible records anyone being filled with the Spirit it is in connection with giving men abilities to do a job. 'See I have chosen Bezalel son of Uri . . . and I have filled him with the Spirit of God, with skill, ability and knowledge in all kinds of crafts—to make artistic designs. . .' (Ex 31:2–4). Knowledge is about ideas, knowing where you are going. Skill is the ability to implement ideas. The Holy Spirit imparted both.

We need both willingness and ability. Being well-meaning is not enough. In fact, the greater the disparity between the willingness and the ability the more dangerous one becomes. Zero ability and zero willingness mean you will not get up to much. You have no motivation to move into a field where you are a bumbler. But zero ability with 100% willingness means you are likely to try your hand and fail in blazing technicolour. Consider a three-year-old who wants to cook breakfast for Daddy. Zero ability with 100% willingness means that you will get scrambled eggs even if they were meant to be fried, and if you do not like jam in your coffee, well, that's bad luck for you. You had just better acquire more catholic tastes.

## How to find your gifts

This book is not on the subject of spiritual gifts, and so a long diversion on just what they are, how they are and where they are, would be inappropriate. However, a summary of how to find our spiritual gifts is relevant to guidance in light of what we have said concerning 'gift theology' above. Here is a useful five step approach:

1. Study what the Bible had to say about the gifts. See the teaching sections, plus take note of how they were used by Jesus and the disciples. Read some of the many good books on the gifts of the Spirit.

2. Experiment. You cannot find your spiritual gift in your study. It's not there, but rather it's in you waiting to be called out by a real life need. You have to get out and try different activities. Go on a summer beach mission or a similar activity and you will find out whether you have a gift in evangelism or not. Get involved in a Bible study and you will find out if you have any gift in teaching. Be part of a prayer group and you will see if you have any leadership gifting. Some things you will find out with a bang that you are not gifted for, but at least you will then know. Happily, you will also find out areas where you are gifted.

Experimenting takes time. That means guidance as to
our calling takes time. Guidance is a process.

3. Ask what you enjoy. Paul says that one aspect of
the will of God is that it is 'pleasing' (Rom 12:2).
Exercising our gifts will not only be pleasing to God and
to others as they are blessed by our gift, but also to
ourselves. The word 'gift' comes from the Greek word
'chara' which means 'joy' or 'gladness'. We will experience a sense of fulfilment as we exercise our gift, a sense
that 'we were made for this'. Indeed we were. Where this
sense of joy and fulfilment is lacking, all things being
equal, there we are probably not operating in our gift.[26]

4. Evaluate your effectiveness. The gifts are task
oriented. They are the means to an end, tools for a job.
If we have a gift it will be evidenced by some sort of
positive result. Of course, we must give room for an
immature gift that needs developing, but even at this
immature stage there will be flashes of effectiveness. If
you often teach and everybody ends up confused, or if
you launch out to lead and look behind and no one is
following, then you need to question if you are moving
in the area of your gifting.

5. Expect confirmation from the body. If you have a
gift then others will notice it. If you are the only one
convinced that you have a certain gift then I would question whether you really have that gift. Even the unsaved
recognised Jesus' gifts. Barnabas, seeing Paul's gifts,
launched him into ministry at Antioch. The reason why 'A
man's gift makes room for him. . .' (Prov 18:16, NASB) is
because others recognise the positive contribution the
man will make and therefore move over to give him room.


## Desires . . . desirable or otherwise

Another important consideration in seeking your career,
besides knowing what you are looking for and recognising
your gifts and abilities, is to check what your desires are.

Desires are not a sure guide to the will of God that need to be automatically obeyed. But neither are they complete distractions that need to be ignored. God does use desires to lead us in his way. For instance, how has God guaranteed the survival of the human race? Of course, he has provided the earth with the necessary food and water, but I am talking about more than that. How did he insure that the human race would eat this life-sustaining food, that they would take what he has given? Not by giving a stern command—'Thou shalt eat'—but by the simple expedient of an appetite; he gave man a desire for food. God also wanted man to multiply and fill the earth. How did he accomplish this purpose? Again, not by thundering forth with a command but by inserting a desire within man, and man enthusiastically obeys.

God's will for the Jews exiled in Persia was for them to return to their land and rebuild the temple. How was this will communicated to King Cyrus whose permission was needed for this daring venture? The answer is that 'the Lord moved the heart of Cyrus King of Persia' (Ezra 1:1). This word 'moved' could equally be translated 'stirred up'. All of a sudden Cyrus got agitated over this Jewish temple business. He could not rest until he saw it accomplished. All this is saying is that God put a strong desire in his heart.

But Cyrus was an unbeliever. Maybe he was deaf to the voice of God. Does God guide believers in this same indirect way—through our feelings? Well, not only did God guide unbelieving Cyrus to repopulate Israel through an implanted desire, but he also guided believing Nehemiah to rebuild Jerusalem through the exact same means. When Nehemiah heard the report of Jerusalem in its devastation, he 'sat down and wept. For some days I mourned and fasted and prayed before the God of heaven' (Neh 1:4). He had no clear directive or word from God. All he had was a strong desire to do something about the situation. But these desires were actually from

God and were God's way of getting Nehemiah going. Nehemiah recognised this later for he said, 'I had not told anyone what my God had put in my heart to do for Jerusalem' (Neh 2:12).

The New Testament confirms that God still works through our desires in Philippians 2:13 where Paul writes, '. . . for it is God who works in you to will and to act according to his good purpose.' God is not just working in the future, not just in heaven, not just in physical miracles—God is actually working inside us to will what he wills! This does not mean that our will is automatically God's will. We need to be more realistic about our heart's potential for evil and selfishness than that. But it does mean that as we truly give ourselves to God we can trust him to be giving us his desires.

Sometimes our desires will lead us in a direction that does not seem to be very spiritual, like being a bank manager or a salesman. But then God sometimes accomplishes his spiritual purposes in an oblique, indirect manner. Consider the case of Cameron Townsend, founder and director for nearly forty-five years of Wycliffe Bible Translators, the largest linguistic organisation in the world with more than 2,000 members. In 1948, while working in Mexico, he took time off from his missionary work to write a biography of a man he much admired, the socialist president of Mexico, Lazaro Cardenas. Some Wycliffe members questioned the wisdom of diverting time from his work to write about a radical statesman who did not profess a personal faith in Jesus. But 'Uncle Cam' admired the man and his stand for justice and the poor. So he went ahead with the book, even if it did not seem directly in line with his missionary call to the tribes. Interestingly, the practical benefits of this book began to show up four years later when it was used to open up the Catholic Philippines to Wycliffe. President Magsaysay said that: 'Townsend's biography of Cardenas has given me a pattern for national reform.'[27] So keen was

Magsaysay on this group that he opened doors for them into Vietnam through his personal recommendation. The book went on to prove instrumental in opening doors into Catholic South American countries formerly closed to Protestant missionaries. Through the biography they saw that here was a North American group that was sympathetic to their plight and viewpoint. So much for the book being a digression. Wycliffe members were then glad that Uncle Cam had followed his desires.

## Guaranteed protection?

How can we be sure that our desires are not leading us away from God's will instead of into it? The answer is not in rules but in relationship, in trust and obedience to God. God is our protection, not our methods. We have to trust him that as we fulfil the conditions to guidance then he will lead us and he will form our desires. He says he will do just that. See Psalm 37:4: 'Delight yourself in the Lord (condition) and he will give you the desires of your heart (promise)', and Romans 12:2: 'Do not conform any longer to the pattern of this world, but be transformed by the renewing of your mind (condition). Then you will be able to test and approve what God's will is. . . .'

There is the promise, and there is the condition. As our minds are renewed we shall not only know God's will but we will approve it; our emotions will come in line with it, saying, 'Hey, that's good.'

God has promised that not only does he work his will out there somewhere but he works his will into us so that we sense it and feel it. His will is not just an outside proposition we give mental assent to, but it becomes part of us, part of our desires. That is what Paul means when he writes, '. . . for it is God who works in you to will and to act according to his good purpose' (Phil 2:13).

What protection do we have against our desires leading us wrongly? God and his promies! If we are seeking him and allowing him to renew our minds God will work for us. The apostle Paul writes, 'All of us who are mature should take such a view of things. And if on some point you think differently, that too God will make clear to you' (Phil 3:15). That's a promise. God is our protection.

This does not mean we will never make mistakes or take wrong turnings, but it does mean God will teach us from our mistakes and turn us back onto the right turnings.


### Diverted or driven

If God has a plan for our lives then so does the devil. Paul says as much in Ephesians 6:11 where he exhorts the believers to 'take your stand against the devil's schemes.' A scheme is a plan, a thought-out strategy of attack. As the devil is not creative but a pure reactionary, he just takes what God desires for us and then attempts to implement the opposite.

He has two techniques to nudge us off the will of God: he will try to drive us, or divert us. In driving us he will push us beyond what God is wanting us to do. His expectations will be higher than God's. He will even come over as more spiritual. This is how he tempted Jesus on the mountain in the desert. He told Jesus to throw himself off the cliff. He even quoted scripture in order to make his suggestion seem God-honouring (Mt 4:6). He insinuated that if Jesus 'really' believed he was God's son then he would do it; he would show his trust in a supernatural Father through a supernatural step (a step off the mountain . . . and a step in the wrong direction).

David Brainerd, a prayer warrior of the 18th century in the early American colonies virtually wore himself out praying for revival among the American Indians. He prayed night and day. He prayed outside in winter for hours until all around him was melted snow, so earnest were his intercessions. And in the end he saw the revival he had prayed for. Brainerd died at the early age of twenty-eight because of his exertions. While he had no regrets for the life he had lived, he did counsel his missionary brother to take more care of himself than he had done. He thought he had been unwise in overexerting himself and that he could have had more years of usefulness had he paced himself better. The devil is a driver, God is not.

## Diverted . . . not driven

But the vast majority of Christians are not in mortal danger of being driven to do more than God wants us to do. Our number one danger is diversion. Jesus, in his exhortation to be ready for the last days, warned his disciples (he is not speaking to the unbelieving world in this passage) of the pitfall of diversion: 'Be careful, or your hearts will be weighed down with dissipation, drunkenness and the anxieties of life, and that day will close on you unexpectedly like a trap' (Lk 21:34). The picture is of a heart weighed down in the concerns of this world and unable to soar up into the concerns of heaven. It cannot soar like an eagle, it can only crawl like a grub. Why? Because it has been diverted away from heavenly aims to earthly pleasures and earthly responsibilities. Notice that it is not just pleasures that are the problem ('dissipation', 'drunkenness'), but responsibilities ('anxieties'). The devil would want to divert us into thinking totally about our own survival or our family's well-being, to the exclusion of the wider call of building his kingdom.

## The self—glorified or crucified

There can be a subtle but deadly shift from desires as indicators of God's will to fulfilling desires as the point of God's will. Instead of seeking God's will with a sense of satisfaction being a sign that we are in God's will, we can just seek satisfaction full stop. 'God wants me to be happy,' becomes our bottom line. Rather than seriously seeking to serve God, we then seek to please ourselves, glibly assuming that what pleases us pleases God. The self is put at the centre rather than God.

This is all the easier to do in our modern age which makes a religion of selfishness. Man has always been selfish, but only recently has he been able to cloak his selfishness, not only with respectability but also with an aura of moral 'progressiveness' and scientific inevitability.

The Bible's command to crucify the self rather than to glorify it is in complete conflict with the spirit of our age. Two literary/intellectual societies—the Bloomsbury Group and the Cambridge Apostles (with members like Bertrand Russell, E M Forster, Lytton Strachey, and later, the Soviet agents Guy Burgess, Anthony Blunt and Leo Long)—were hugely influential on the intellectual climate of the 1920s and 1930s. Central in their thinking was a swing away from the Victorian concepts of 'duty'. The self was more important than society; relationships were more important than conventional, absolute morality. As E M Forster wrote, 'If I had to choose between betraying my country and betraying my friend, I hope I should have the guts to betray my country.' The 1960s so successfully continued in this vein that it was tagged 'the me decade'. 'If it feels good, do it,' rang out the new anthem. The sixties have been left behind, but its spirit remains.

The 'psychologised' 20th century has, perhaps, taken the self more seriously than any of the previous centuries. The self has been analysed, scrutinised and glorified. 'To thine own self be true,' replaced self-sacrifice as the new golden rule. The new morality suggested new models of virtue, and they were meant, despite appearances, to be taken seriously. Here is one example:

Fidelity . . . is redefined in open marriage, as commitment to your own growth, equal commitment to your partner's growth, and a sharing of the self-discovery accomplished through such growth. It is loyalty and faithfulness to growth, to integrity and to self and respect for the other, not to a sexual and psychological bondage to each other.

In an open marriage, in which each partner is secure in his own identity and trusts in the other, new possibilities for additional relationships exist, and open (as opposed to limited) love can expand to include others. . . . These outside relationships may, of course, include sex.[28]

Of course! One only wonders why the authors took so long in coming around to saying what they really wanted to say. So now adultery, debauchery and immorality are actually expressions of integrity and love. Up is down, and down is up; just wave the wand of self-growth. The aroma of complete cant oozes from every pore of this philosophy, but a world enamoured with self knows no better. For those who believe in the garden serpent with his oily insinuations, it is all déjà vu. We have heard it all before.

## Slippery motives

If we are to use our desires as an indicator of the direction in which we should go, then we need to distinguish between totally selfish desires and God-glorifying desires. This is easier said than done because we are talking about hidden motives rather than concrete actions. Two actions can look exactly the same on the outside and yet one be virtuous and the other non-virtuous. The difference is in the motive. And yet motives are slippery things to get a hold of. Think of the following:

Paul—even a self-sacrificing, heroic defender of the faith like the apostle Paul could have had his motives doubted. One could have easily accused him of doing everything from a spirit of one-upmanship, selfish ambition, glossed over with a convincing veneer of spirituality.

David—David's motives in challenging Goliath not only *could* have been questioned but *were* by his brothers who said, 'I know how conceited you are and how wicked your heart is; you came down only to watch the battle' (1 Sam 17:28).

Jesus—yes, even Jesus' motives were open to suspicion. His brothers said to him, ' "No-one who wants to become a public figure acts in secret. Since you are doing these things, show yourself to the world." For even his own brothers did not believe in him' (Jn 7:4–5). Jesus' drive in serving his Father could have been mistaken for selfish ambition. The outer expression of drive—a drive for God or a drive for self—is often the same. But the inner motivations are poles apart.

## Purifying motives

In the absence of a made-to-measure objective standard that will clearly prove our motives for an action, is there anything we can do to protect and develop godly motivation? Yes, indeed. Here are my suggestions:

1. Consecrate yourselves wholly to God.
2. Pray.
3. Seek to serve now.

'Consecration theology' has got it exactly right when it says, according to Romans 12:1, that the first step in knowing the will of God is to give ourselves wholly to God. To be a Christian means that we seek first the kingdom of God. We are here to serve God and we need to give ourselves to this end. Our chief goal cannot be getting ahead (keeping up with the Jones's escalates into the rat race, otherwise known as 'buying things you don't need with money you don't have to keep up with people you don't like'), personal fulfilment or security. These elements come into our decisions, but they must not be allowed to have the final say.

Of course, our purely personal desires do not enter our decisions. When I choose cornflakes over Weetabix for breakfast it is not because 'cornflakes will bring greater glory to God,' but simply because I like cornflakes better. But underlying everything must be a heart that beats with a desire to see God glorified. This will mean that while I am free in the main to choose cornflakes I may have to forego that pleasure for a greater good—for instance, for a fast day, or if I go to serve in a foreign country where they have no cornflakes (gadzooks!). Service over self-fulfilment is the Christian's way. 'Whoever finds his life will lose it, and whoever loses his life for my sake will find it,' is what Jesus said (Mt 10:39).

How different is this motivation from the world around us. In a book like Jeffrey Archer's *First Among Equals*, an excellent novel about four capable men aspiring for political careers, the whole question is, 'Which one will make it?' Political service is seen as a step-ladder to career greatness. The aspect of politics as service to one's country is lost in the quest for the ultimate, glittering prize of political ambition: being prime minister. Ironically minister means servant, so that prime minister was originally intended to convey that this office was the foremost servant in the country. It is all too easy to slip into this mentality, even in obviously Christian careers like preaching or being a missionary.

## It's as simple as one, two, three

How do we consecrate ourselves? Firstly, by choosing to do so. It is that simple. Joshua challenged his people, '. . . choose for yourselves this day whom you will serve, whether the gods your forefathers served beyond the river, or the gods of the Amorites, in whose land you are living. But as for me and my household, we will serve the

Lord' (Josh 24:15). Joshua seemed to think that it was as simple as a choice that they could make right there and then. So it is. Choose to give yourself to God. Secondly, ask God to work in your heart to preserve and deepen this commitment. We need God even in our choices. This is what the psalmist did in Psalm 119:36 where he writes, 'Turn my heart towards your statutes and not towards selfish gain.' Asked sincerely, this is the kind of prayer God loves to answer. It is a prayer after his own heart.

Prayer was the second safeguard. As we spend time in prayer, God is free to speak to us and show us if we are straying from his ways. 'He who seeks finds,' Jesus promised (Mt 7:8). The context here is prayer. If we seek his will in prayer (our part) then he will show us his will as opposed to ours (God's part).

Active service now is the third safeguard. The saying, 'It is easier to steer a moving ship than a stationary one,' is altogether true. As God's will for us involves service, the earlier we get involved in service the closer we will be to the heart of God and the more easily we will hear from him. Rather than awaiting a heavenly vision we can get involved where we are in some form of practical service. This could mean financial giving, practical help to old people, giving spiritual counselling, or taking the childrens' Sunday school. Get involved. In every situation we can choose to opt in or opt out. The latter is not really an 'option'. Countless times the command to serve is linked with the command to worship. You cannot separate them. If there really exists an inner heart disposition to worship there will be, of necessity, a desire to serve right alongside it. As we reach out in service we will begin to see what areas God anoints and what gifts we have. We will begin to see more clearly what God has for us.

## Art versus science

Guidance is more an art than a science. To get the desired result in the laboratory you simply combine the correct ingredients in the prescribed dosages, and then get the prescribed results. Art is not like that; it does not come out in prescribed dosages. It is more spontaneous and surprising, and it takes more 'feel'. Guidance is not a science operating according to rigid rules but is an art whose principles cannot be woodenly applied outside of a living relationship with God.

We know God guides by his voice, through reason and feelings, and through our own initiatives. Which method comes into play at what time is not a matter to be worked out by strict rules but as we work out our relationship with God, as he unfolds how he wants to communicate his will to us. It is not a matter of throwing thirty-three per cent supernatural guidance, thirty-three per cent reason, and thirty-three per cent personal initiative into each decision. Nor does God simplify matters by saying, 'What we'll do is this: I will bring revelations to you from 6am till noon, your own reason should be used from noon till 6pm, and go ahead and use your creative sense in the evening.'

But neither does God lead us into the same quandary that Somerset Maugham left his listeners in when he said, 'There are three basic rules on how to write a novel. The problem is nobody knows what they are.' No, God does show us the way forward.

God shows us that he speaks, how he speaks, and how we can hear him. Through his promises he reaches out to us to motivate us to listen to him. We have more than the hope of guidance—we have the promise of guidance.

It is now up to us to take God up on his word and discover the adventure of guidance. Man walking with a personal God who wants to personally direct his life! God will teach us the art of guidance. He who gave us the tools will teach us how to wield them. It matters not whether we are highly skilled at this art for God is, and he will hold the paint-brush with us.

'The Father . . . will give you another Counsellor. . . he lives with you and will be in you . . . the Counsellor. . . will teach you all things. . .' (John 14:16–17, 26).

# Notes

1. A W Tozer, *The Pursuit of God* (Kingsway Publications: Eastbourne, 1984).

2. A W Tozer, *The Root of the Righteous* (Christian Publications: Harrisburg, Pennsylvania, USA, 1955).

3. Morton T Kelsey, *Healing and Christianity* (Harper & Row: New York, 1973).

4. Please note that this prophecy that Paul refers to is not 'exhortatory preaching' or preaching 'revved up'; that would be unfair to the way in which this word is consistently used throughout the Old and New Testaments. That more than teaching is meant by this word is plain from 1 Corinthians 12:28 where the prophet is differentiated from the teacher, and 1 Corinthians 14:25 shows that the revelation of secrets rather than systematic teaching is its hallmark (of such a supernatural degree that an unbeliever is convinced of the existence of the Christian's God). Also, 1 Corinthians 14:30–32 speaks of spontaneous revelations rather than premeditated studies.

5. A W Tozer, *The Root of the Righteous*.

6. *Leadership: A Practical Journal for Church Leaders* (Winter 1983): p. 82.

7. Arnold Dallimore, *George Whitefield: The Life and Times of the Great Evangelist of the Eighteenth Century Revival* (Banner of Truth: Edinburgh, 1970).

8. J I Packer, *Knowing God* (Hodder & Stoughton: London, 1975).

9. It is not so clear that 'intuition is fallible but spiritual'.

Clearly intuition is fallible, but is it also 'spiritual' in the sense usually understood? Something spiritual usually denotes something supernatural as opposed to something natural. But is the exercise of our intuition anything more than a natural function? Consider that many scientific advances are the result of intuition—of following hunches. Are these necessarily the voice of God? I think not. Intuition is a natural faculty placed within man and is no more spiritual than emotion or reason. One would hesitate to call Edison's invention of the light bulb a spiritual breakthrough. It wasn't, even though it involved the use of intuition. In the usual sense, then, intuition is not spiritual.

10. Kenneth E Hagin, *How You Can Be Led by the Spirit of God* (Rhema Bible Church: Tulsa, Oklahoma, USA, 1978).

11. Watchman Nee, *The Spiritual Man* (3 vols) (STL Trust: Bromley, 1968).

12. *ibid*.

13. *ibid*.

14. *ibid*.

15. It is interesting to note that Watchman Nee himself concluded that this teaching was impractical and therefore asked for *The Spiritual Man* not to be reprinted (see *What Shall This Man Do?*, Victory Press, 1961, pp. vii–viii). However, he still stood by the theory of what he said, and the book was reprinted and continues in circulation today.

16. Hagin, *op. cit*.

17. We want to avoid terminological confusion, but we also want to avoid terminological paranoia. Paranoia is what you get as you face this onslaught of pseudo-technical labels. Terminological paranoia is that state of mind sometimes known to afflict novices in the Bible when they find themselves afraid to use a theological term for fear of being caught out by biblical scholars and experts. I am certainly not advocating that we aim for a scientific accuracy in our language, saying things like, 'What a spiritual-in-sense-one person.' This is absurdly unnatural and stilted. In achieving preciseness of meaning we sacrifice grace. A degree of looseness of terms is altogether natural in our ordinary speech.

18. Norman Cousins, 'The Miracle of Creativity', *Leadership: A Practical Journal for Church Leaders*, vol 4, no 1.

19. W I B Beveridge, *The Art of Scientific Investigation* (Vintage Books: New York, USA).

20. *ibid*.

21. *ibid*.

22. *ibid*.

23. *ibid*.

24. Francis A Schaeffer, *The Church at the End of the Twentieth Century* (Norfolk Press: London, 1972).

25. Norman Vincent Peale, *The Power of Positive Thinking* (Ballantine Books: New York, 1982).

26. I say 'all things being equal' because our lack of joy can arise from a number of sources. We may be exercising our gift and yet in our hearts we may be grumbling against God, against doing his will. Perhaps we are shying away from the cost of doing his will and exercising our gifts. Renewed commitment to the Lord, not a change of ministry, is the solution here. We are miserable because we are not surrendered.

27. James and Marti Hefley, *Uncle Cam* (Mott Media: Milford, Michigan, USA, 1981).

28. Nena and George O'Neill, *Open Marriage: A New Life Style for Couples* (P Owen: London, 1973).

For further information about Youth With A Mission in the United Kingdom, please write to:

Youth With A Mission
13 Highfield Oval, Ambrose Lane, Harpenden, Hertfordshire AL5 4BX. Tel. 0582 65481

# Is That Really You, Lord?

**by Loren Cunningham**

As a young man, Loren Cunningham was given a startling vision of waves of young people moving out across the continents, spreading the gospel to a needy and rebellious world.

What did the vision mean? Was it telling him about the future? Was it from God?

In the birth of Youth With a Mission we see how hearing the voice of God can lead to great blessing if we are ready to obey Him in complete trust. As we see how God prepared Loren to tap the energies of young people for the gospel, we are encouraged to look for more of God's supernatural guidance in our own lives.

Loren Cunningham is Director of Youth With a Mission. He lives in Hawaii with his wife and two children. Janice Rogers is Loren's sister and a professional writer.

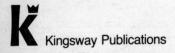
Kingsway Publications

# Intimate Friendship with God

## by Joy Dawson

'Every person is either fulfilled or frustrated to the degree he or she is in intimate friendship with God.'

Can we really know God as an intimate friend? And if so, what is the key to such a relationship?

At a time when so many are after instant gratification, Joy Dawson reminds us of 'the fear of the Lord'. This, she says, is the hallmark of intimate friendship with God. As we learn to love the truth that He loves, and to hate the sin that He hates, we become recognizable as His people. We begin to 'delight in holiness'. And He delights in us . . .

The price is high, but the privileges and rewards still higher.

**Joy Dawson** has taught with Youth With A Mission in over forty countries and her ministry has been enjoyed by thousands seeking a deeper experience of God. She and her husband Jim have two married children.

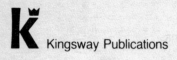

Kingsway Publications

# Preparing for Battle

## by Peter Adams

*'For our struggle is not against flesh and blood,
but against the rulers, against the authorities,
against the powers of this dark world, and against
the spiritual forces of evil in the heavenly realms'*
(Eph 6:12 NIV).

What has spiritual warfare to do with the area in which
you live, the rest of your community and its history?
And what can Christians *do* to make a difference to the
spiritual climate in which they live?

Peter Adams has spent several years researching his
local area—London—while working with Youth With
A Mission. In that time he has learnt to blend biblical
insights with local knowledge as a base from which to
carry out the reclaiming of lost ground from the enemy.
The result is a practical source book as well as a
thoughtful apologetic for spiritual warfare.

*'A unique, practical study of this important subject'*
—LYNN GREEN, Director, Youth With A Mission
(Europe, Middle East, Africa)

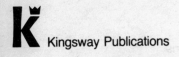

Kingsway Publications